"This book is an absolute unicornucopia of magic, delicious delight, and an enjoyable education on all things cake baking and decorating. Unicorn-approved!"

–JESSIE OLESON MOORE, CakeSpy.com

. . . .

"*Erin Bakes Cake* is a modern mash-up of fundamental baking techniques and creative genius. Erin breaks down the nitty gritty details of baking success with relatable charm, whimsical diagrams, rainbow charts, and a heavy sprinkling of fun. In the world of baking books, this one is truly a unicorn."

–CARRIE SELLMAN, founder of TheCakeBlog.com

. . . .

"Erin is in baking and with cakes what I try to be in DIY: a fun, 'you can do this' approach that makes it easy to achieve the things you want. This must-get book will have you making cake for days!"

–NICOLE FARB, founder of *Darby Smart*

. . . .

"Ordinary cake books are fine for all those other boring bakers out there, but you want to be like me: a culinary rebel who plays by their own rules! Erin Gardner will help show you the way: This technicolor tome will help you unleash the buttery beast, letting you follow your heart to the cake of your dreams."

–ALLISON ROBICELLI, chef, James Beard award nominee and author of *Robicelli's: A Love Story, with Cupcakes*

ERIN
BAKES
CAKE

Variation of
Lux Layers Cake
(page 197)

ERIN BAKES CAKE

MAKE + BAKE + DECORATE =
YOUR OWN CAKE ADVENTURE!

ERIN GARDNER

RODALE.

RODALE
wellness

Live happy. Be healthy. Get inspired.

Sign up today to get exclusive access to our authors, exclusive bonuses,
and the most authoritative, useful, and cutting-edge information on health,
wellness, fitness, and living your life to the fullest.

Visit us online at RodaleWellness.com
Join us at RodaleWellness.com/Join

Rodale books may be purchased for business of promotional use for special sales.
For information, please email rodalebooks@rodale.com.

Printed in China

Rodale Inc. makes every effort to use acid-free ♾, recycled paper ♻.

**Photographs pages ii, v, x, xiii, 1, 4, 8, 9, 16, 22, 26, 27, 36, 54, 91–94, 101, 102, 106, 121,
126, 130, 138, 143, 178, 185, 190, 202, 206, 210, 214, 216–218, 220, 228–230, 242**
Photography by Mitch Mandel/Rodale Images
Prop styling by Stephanie Hanes

**Photographs pages 7, 10, 13, 28, 31, 35, 43, 52, 78, 105, 108, 110, 112–114, 116, 118, 119, 123, 124, 127,
128, 131, 132, 134, 136, 139, 140, 145, 147, 148, 150, 153, 155, 157, 158, 161, 163, 165, 166, 168, 170,
173, 174, 176, 179, 180, 187, 188, 191, 193, 195, 196, 198, 201, 203, 204, 207, 209, 212, 215, 221**
Photography by Heath Robbins
Prop styling by Verne Cordova

Photograph page xi
Photography by Michael Woytek

Emoji icons: flower travelin' man/Shutterstock

Sprinkle pattern: AlfaSmart/Shutterstock

Illustrations by Gabriella Sanchez

Book design by Rae Ann Spitzenberger

Library of Congress Cataloging-in-Publication Data is on file with the publisher.

ISBN-13: 978–1–62336–836–4   hardcover

Distributed to the trade by Macmillan

2   4   6   8   10   9   7   5   3   1

Follow us @RodaleBooks on

We inspire health, healing, happiness, and love in the world.
Starting with you.

*For Mike, Maxwell,
and Violet. Hearts.*

CONTENTS

PART 2

piece of cake

PART 3

eye candy

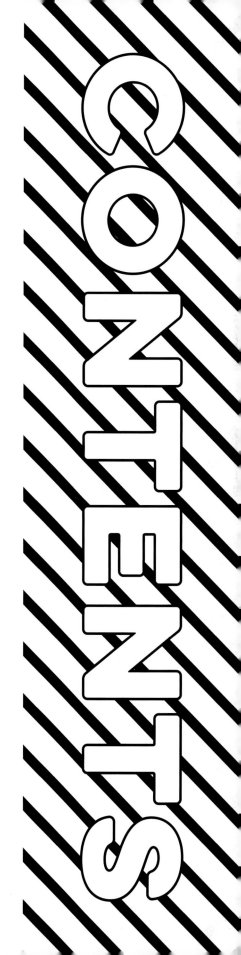

Clockwise from top:
Wedding Bells Cake (page 208);
Pretty Kitty Cake, rainbow variation (page 157);
Sweet Bouquet Cake (page 114)

MEET YOUR baker

THIS IS GOING TO BE FUN.

There are many things you are required to do with your time that are not fun: laundry, taking the garbage out, paying taxes, etc. We have many of these un-fun, time-consuming demands in our lives. When you choose to spend some of your precious free time baking, it should be fun. Lots of fun!

Fun is a relative term, though. I know for some fun is getting from point A (recipe) to point B (delicious cake), in the shortest amount of time possible. For others, fun is digging into the baking process and executing recipes as precisely as possible. This book is for both types. I know I fall into either one of those categories depending on how much time I have and who I'm baking for.

WHO AM I TO TELL YOU HOW TO BAKE A CAKE?

The nerve, right? It's actually a great question. Recipes are a dime a dozen these days, so you need to know which ones you can trust.

Cake has ruled my baking world for many years now. I started the sweet life working as a professional pastry chef and eventually opening my award-winning wedding cake shop, Wild Orchid Baking Company, in North Hampton, NH. In my time at the bakery, *Martha Stewart Weddings* and *Brides* magazines both named my shop one of the best in the country. I trucked my tools down to NYC to compete on Food Network's *Sweet Genius*—and I won! (Thank you very much baby food and horseradish.) Seven years and two babies later, I decided it was time to bid my wedding couples adieu and move on to the next

hi, i'm erin →

stage in my cakey-bakey career. I've continued to share my baking and pastry knowledge through blogging and teaching.

Any Cake, Who?

My cake recipes are unique. They're "Any" recipes. Why have one recipe for pumpkin spice cake and another recipe for strawberry cake, when you can have one recipe that works with either puree? You won't find six dozen recipes here that *kind of* do the same thing with a different ingredient here or there. Each recipe is loaded with delicious variations. I'm sharing the efficient techniques I learned through baking in restaurants and at my bakery for you to use in your own home.

Mmmm, Creamy

Cake loves frosting. And frosting loves cake. It's a match made in heaven. The recipes in the Creamy chapter do double duty as both filling and frosting options.

You could even make one buttercream, divide it in half, make each half a different flavor using one of the listed variations, and then use one as a filling and the other as a frosting. Blew your mind just now, didn't I?

What the Crunch?

In my chef-y days, I focused on creating plated desserts that were balanced in terms of both flavor and texture. Moving into the cake world, I apply that same thought process to create layer cakes that consist of tender cake, creamy fillings, and an element of crunch. Sometimes the crunch is on the outside, sometimes on the inside, but it's always there. The recipes in the Crunchy chapter can be chopped up and added to cake layers, folded into buttercream or cake batter before baking, or used to decorate cakes.

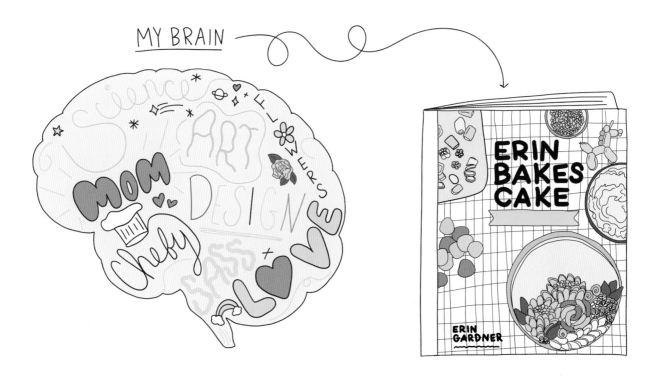

No Fondant?

Nope, not this time. In recent years I've ditched the rolled stuff and challenged myself to develop cake decorating techniques that mimic the polished style of fondant cakes, but with elements that are beautiful *and* delicious. Candy, cookie doughs, and chocolate are my design mediums of choice. Don't get me wrong, fondant has its place. I built a fancy-schmancy wedding cake business around the stuff. But for everyday occasions, it's just not practical. It takes a great deal of time, practice, and counter space to roll fondant that's thin and delicate, as opposed to thick and gummy. I've been rolling fondant for years and it still stresses me out. It's the spandex minidress of the cake world: totally unforgiving and reveals all flaws. When I'm at home, I want a cake that I can run past and scoop up a finger full of frosting as I'm chasing the kids around, not a precious confection that I know is silently judging me.

WHY I BAKE

I think cake is kind of a big deal. At birthday parties, we don't take pictures of kids in front of a salad. Crowds of people don't gather 'round a newlywed couple to watch them lovingly slice into a turkey. Cake does more than make people happy; it helps us mark the celebrations in our lives with a little bit of shared sweetness.

My favorite part of being a wedding cake designer was that people came to my shop during the most exciting times in their lives, wanting to include my cakes in their celebrations. People loved my shop's cakes because there was more to them than just

sugar, butter, flour, and eggs. I thoughtfully combined flavors and textures, and changed them seasonally, to fully take advantage of and celebrate the bounty of available ingredients here in New Hampshire. I built trust with my clients through their taste buds and then wowed them with meticulous design.

My favorite part about baking now is being able to draw on those professional accomplishments to enhance the baking I do at home with my kids. There are so many similarities between being a pastry chef and managing a home. You learn to make do with what you have, to take everyday things and elevate them to something that's extraordinary. In sharing these experiences, I bring the same loving care and attention to detail from my cake shop days to now teaching people how to bake and decorate masterpieces of their own.

PART 1

bake without breaking a sweat

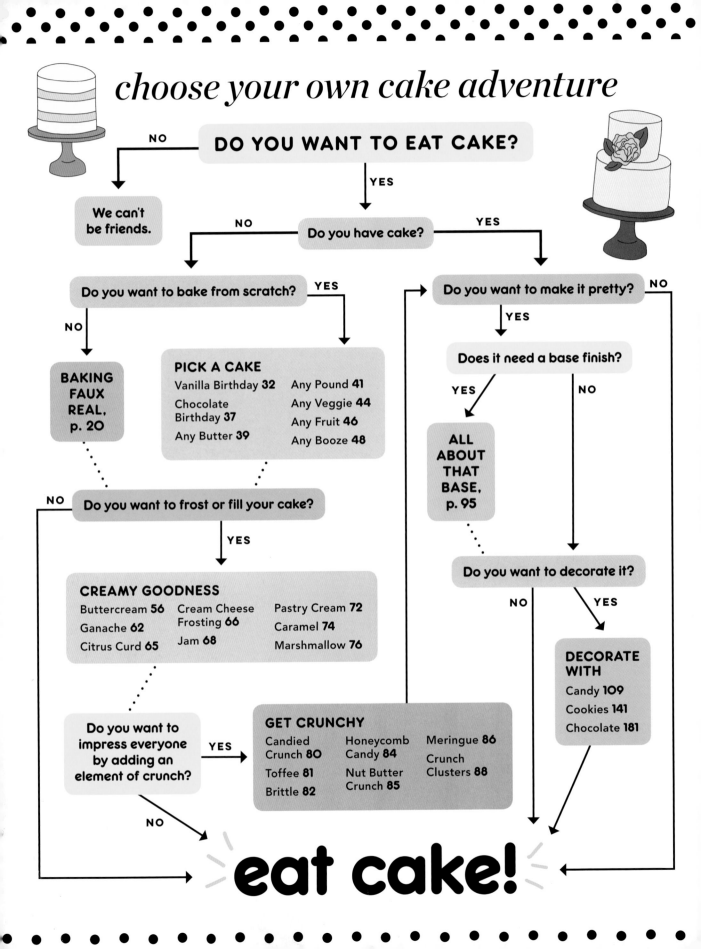

choose your own cake adventure

DO YOU WANT TO EAT CAKE?

NO → We can't be friends.

YES → **Do you have cake?**

NO → **Do you want to bake from scratch?**

NO → **BAKING FAUX REAL, p. 20**

YES → **PICK A CAKE**
Vanilla Birthday **32**
Chocolate Birthday **37**
Any Butter **39**
Any Pound **41**
Any Veggie **44**
Any Fruit **46**
Any Booze **48**

Do you want to frost or fill your cake?

YES → **CREAMY GOODNESS**
Buttercream **56**
Ganache **62**
Citrus Curd **65**
Cream Cheese Frosting **66**
Jam **68**
Pastry Cream **72**
Caramel **74**
Marshmallow **76**

Do you want to impress everyone by adding an element of crunch?

YES → **GET CRUNCHY**
Candied Crunch **80**
Toffee **81**
Brittle **82**
Honeycomb Candy **84**
Nut Butter Crunch **85**
Meringue **86**
Crunch Clusters **88**

NO →

YES → **Do you want to make it pretty?** NO →

YES → **Does it need a base finish?**

YES → **ALL ABOUT THAT BASE, p. 95**

NO →

Do you want to decorate it?

NO →

YES → **DECORATE WITH**
Candy **109**
Cookies **141**
Chocolate **181**

eat cake!

HOW TO USE THIS BOOK

while on your cakey adventure, you may ask yourself ...

I wonder what that (cake, frosting, cookie, etc.) looks like in a cake slice?

I'm so glad you wondered that. I love to look at pretty pictures of cake slices, too. That's why I filled a book with them. Yay! Look for the "See It In a Slice" notes to find page numbers corresponding to the picture of the recipe you're ogling.

Oooh, that sounds good, but I don't have time to bake from scratch. What should I do?

Don't panic! Your box mix secrets are safe with me. **DOCTOR, DOCTOR!** is here to save the day with store-bought alternatives listed within most recipes. These tidbits have also been gathered up into one place as a handy-dandy reference guide, Baking Faux Real (page 20).

That's a pretty cake decoration thingy. I want something similar, but I don't have much time, because I just remembered it's my (insert loved one's name here) birthday. Today.

I feel your pain. I'm a procrastination monkey, myself. Look for **FAUX FABULOUS** decorating ideas within many of the decorating projects or head straight to the Candy section starting on page 109.

I wonder what would go perfectly with that (cake, frosting, filling, etc.)?

OMG, I'm flattered. I'm honored that you would trust my taste buds with your important cake decisions. Turn to page 50 for the **PERFECT PAIRINGS** of your cakey dreams.

What would a unicorn do?

I ask myself that on the daily. A real life unicorn was consulted during the writing of this book. Her tips and musings can be found sprinkled throughout the book under **UNICORN THOUGHTS.** (OK, you got me. I'm the unicorn. Find out why on page 189.)

UNICORN thought

Chapter 1

THE GOODS

BAKING, FILLING, AND DECORATING A CAKE REQUIRES practice, patience, and *the goods*. Your cakey tasks will quickly move from tedious chore to enjoyable pastime when you use the right tools for the job. The equipment and brands I mention in this section are things I use all the time. The photos are of my actual tools, straight from the box. (Well, after a little bath and polish.) Since picking up cake baking and decorating as a hobby or profession requires an investment in specialized tools and ingredients, it's important to know which ones work best in order to save yourself time, money, and frustration.

If I could wave a magic wand and go back in time, my advice to baby-Erin would be: Buy nice to avoid buying twice. I blew through more cheap-o measuring cup sets and wobbly plastic turntables than I like to admit. Learn from my misplaced frugality and treat yo' self.

TOOLS OF THE TRADE

Stand Mixer

I use a KitchenAid, as do many other pros and home bakers. They last forever if you take care of them and make very light work of labor-intensive jobs like creaming butter and whipping egg whites. If you plan on baking a lot, you may want to pick up extra stand-mixer bowls so you can easily move from recipe to recipe without having to stop and wash the bowl. You can also use the second bowl to prep the next recipe you want to work on while another one is working on the mixer.

Mixing Bowls

Keep a variety of sizes on hand for small jobs like separating eggs and large jobs like making big batches of batter. Purchase bowls that are heatproof, so they can do double duty over a double boiler. I always have at least one microwave-safe bowl in my pantry, too.

Rubber Spatulas

Solid, heatproof, silicone spatulas are the most versatile and easiest to clean.

Measuring Spoons

My favorite set of spoons are Williams Sonoma's narrow measuring spoons. They're long and thin with a flat edge, perfect for getting down to the bottom of narrow spice jars. Plus, they come with an 1/8-teaspoon measure, the ideal size when you just need a smidge of something.

Measuring Cups

Always use dry for dry ingredients and wet for wet ingredients. Large glass measuring cups, like the ones made by Pyrex, are also great for mixing small batches of batter or melting things in the microwave.

Look for dry measuring cups made by a reputable kitchenware company that have solidly attached handles. I was a serial measuring-cup killer (snapping off handles and denting cups) until I finally bit the bullet and sprang for a top-notch set. My all-time favorite cups are made by All-Clad. Super bonus, they're adorable and look like a teeny tiny set of All-Clad pans. Novelty measuring cups in random shapes aren't to be trusted. (Sorry, cute nesting dolls and flower-shaped cups!)

Baking Strips

Baking strips can be found in the cake aisle at most craft stores. You use them by soaking them in water and wrapping them around a cake pan before it goes into the oven. The damp wrap keeps the outer edge of the cake cool so that it bakes at the same rate as the cake batter in the center of the pan. These are by no means 100 percent necessary, but they are pretty cool to have if you bake on a regular basis. You'll end up with flatter cakes with a softer crust that are easier to handle and require less leveling.

Scale

Weighing ingredients is the most accurate way to bake. But if you've been baking with cups and spoons for 30 years with great success, then don't mess with a good thing. Scales are handy to have on hand for weighing random bits of butter and chocolate chips.

Candy Thermometer

Look for one that comes with a clip for attaching the thermometer to the side of your pan. The newer digital ones are great— they'll beep when you reach the temperature you're looking for, saving you from having to stand next to the pot and watch the mercury rise.

Cake Pans

I like tall pans and I cannot lie. All of my cake pans are 3-inch-tall, light-colored aluminum pans. Light-colored pans conduct less heat, so they're less likely to give your cakes a dark crust. Tall pans are also more versatile because you have the room to bake as little or as much batter as you like.

Cookie Sheets

Rimmed, light-colored aluminum cookie sheets are the most useful to have. A lighter color means the pan is less likely to turn the bottoms of your cookies black. Rimmed baking sheets are safer to use and are great for containing messes.

Cooling Racks

These are nice to have, especially when baking in a small space. Cakes and sheets of cookies can be stacked on racks to cool.

Parchment Paper

Frankly, rolls of parchment paper are annoying and often more trouble than they're worth to use. The paper is difficult to handle, curls, and can cause cookies or decorations to become misshapen. Boxes of flat, precut sheets of parchment paper can be inexpensively purchased online and in restaurant supply stores.

Silicone Baking Mats

These are perfect for baking more delicate items, like meringue cookies, that may stick to a greased cookie sheet or parchment paper. They're versatile, typically heatproof to over 450°F, and will last forever if you take care of them.

Icing Spatula

Acetate

Clear, flexible sheets of plastic are ideal for working with chocolate. The slick surface leaves chocolate work with a gorgeous sheen. Sheets or rolls of acetate can be found in specialty chef supply stores and online. They're a one-time-use item, but worth the hassle to find if you're making something special or have an interest in chocolate work.

Dishers or Portion Scoops

If you're not down with the dishers already, it's about time you get to know them. Dishers are portion scoops used in commercial kitchens to ensure uniformity in measuring. They come in all different sizes and are sold in restaurant supply stores and online. Each one has a different colored handle indicating the volume of the scoop. Larger dishers are perfect for filling cupcake liners or dividing batter evenly between pans. Smaller dishers make great cookie and truffle scoops. Ask a pastry chef what their favorite disher is and I'm certain you'll get a response. I'm a green-handle (size 12, 2⅔-ounce) girl, myself.

Piping Bags

Large, plastic disposable piping bags are the most useful to keep in your decorating toolbox. You can cut them down if a smaller bag is better for the job.

Piping Tips and Couplers

Every brand numbers its tips differently, so pay attention more to the size and shape tip that you need. Round, star, leaf, and rose tips are the most common tips. Each can be used in a number of ways to fill, finish, and decorate a cake with very little piping expertise.

Couplers come in two parts. The larger part is placed inside a piping bag before filling it with frosting or meringue. The smaller outer ring is tightened over the coupler and piping bag to hold a tip securely in place. Couplers make switching tips a breeze, and you don't have to constantly empty and refill piping bags.

Icing Spatulas

Offset and straight icing spatulas are the two most commonly used in cake decorating. I keep a large and small one of each on hand when filling and finishing cakes. My preference is for spatulas with plastic handles because they are easier to keep clean. Some people have strong feelings about which spatula should be used for which decorating task (filling, crumb coating, etc.). I say use whatever you're most comfortable with.

Turntable

This is the best cake investment you will ever make, even more so than a stand mixer. A good turntable will enable you to get the smoothest buttercream finishes in the shortest amount of time. I've had the same Ateco turntable for over 10 years. Take care of it and it will last for a lifetime.

Rolling Pins

Everyone's rolling pin preferences are different, so use the kind that's most comfortable for you. I prefer a wooden, straight French-style pin because I feel it gives me greater control over rolling doughs to the desired thickness. Pins with handles separate from the roller can have minds of their own. I feel like I'm one step removed from the dough and have to constantly check it. I also use a similarly shaped plastic pin when I'm rolling doughs or candy that need to be perfectly smooth.

Knives

I've always kept three knives in my toolbox—no more, no less. The first is a standard chef's knife, perfect for cutting larger quantities of fruit or making long cuts into dough. Next is my sharp paring knife, used for making smaller, more precise cuts. My final and favorite knife is a Wüsthof offset serrated knife. The handle is offset from the blade, making it the ideal tool for slicing cake or chopping chocolate and nuts. No smashing your knuckles on the cutting board with every chop.

Paintbrushes

Purchase individually wrapped brushes at the craft store, definitely not ones that are loose in a bin. Brushes with white synthetic bristles are the easiest to clean. Because they're white, they allow you to better see how much color or chocolate is on your brush.

Cookie Cutters

Metal cookie cutters are the most versatile because you can use them cold to cleanly cut doughs, or in the oven as a mold for melted candy. 3D printers have totally opened up the cookie cutter world. If you can dream it, someone online can turn it into a relatively inexpensive cookie cutter for you. 3D-printed cutters do have their limitations because they're made of plastic. They typically cannot be submerged in water for very long and are definitely *not* oven-safe.

Cake Boards

Build your cake on a cake board if you plan to place it on a platter or cake stand with a lip, or if you don't have room in your fridge to store a cake on a stand. Cardboard cake rounds are sold in the same diameters as cake pans. Larger boards can be cut to fit unusually shaped cakes. Find them at craft stores and big box stores, or purchase online.

Candy
Shapes

Rock Candy

Dragées

Quins

Pearl
Sugar

Sugar
Crystals

Sprinkles

Sanding Sugar

Nonpareils

Sugar Pearls

Unicorn
Poop

SPRINKLE GUIDE

Sprinkles

AKA: *Jimmies; Sugar Strands; Heaven in a Jar (amirite?!)*

Sprinkles are long, thin, pleasantly crunchy bits of unicorn tears (or a combination of sugar, starches, colorings, and flavors wrapped in a thin carnauba wax shell). Rainbow assorted and chocolate are the most common varieties. *Sprinkles* is also a general term that describes any sort of tiny candy or confection used to decorate a dessert. I first fell in love with rainbow sprinkles at Magnifico's Ice Cream in East Brunswick, NJ. Their vanilla soft-serve in a waffle cone topped with rainbow sprinkles would be my death-row dessert.

Nonpareils

AKA: *Hundreds-and-thousands*

Nonpareils are sprinkles' itsy-bitsy, round, and slightly crunchier cousins. The French word *nonpareil* loosely translates as "without equal." Chocolates coated in these round candies are also referred to as nonpareils.

Sugar Pearls

AKA: *Sugar Beads*

Larger and crunchier than nonpareils, but typically smaller than gumballs, sugar pearls come in many sizes, colors, and finishes. They're a huge time-saver when creating cake designs that call for a dot pattern. Opening a jar of sugar pearls beats rolling out a million tiny balls of fondant by hand any day of the week.

Dragées

These sleek, lustrous, hard-as-hell confections come in a variety of shapes, sizes, and metallic finishes. Pearl dragées are the most common, but they can also be found in the shape of triangles, hearts, batons, squares, and more. Most metallic dragées are no longer considered food-safe here in the US and are sold to be used for decorative purposes only. In other parts of the world, they throw caution to the wind and indulge in a shiny, tooth-shattering treat every now and then.

Though most cake decorators would point to the metallic variety when asked to pick a dragée out of a lineup, the term actually applies to any tiny, decorative candy with a hard, crunchy shell. Jordan almonds, Sixlets, and even M&M's are all examples of dragées.

Quins

AKA: *Confetti Quins; Sprinkle Quins; Confetti; Sequins*

These shaped sprinkles are available in a large assortment of colors and forms. They are similar in texture to classic sprinkles, but with a matte finish. Some are flavored to match their theme, like peppermint candy canes.

Candy Shapes

Candy shapes ride the fine line between sprinkles and, well, candy. They're hard on the outside, but crumble into a sugary powder almost immediately upon being bitten into. Candy shapes look fantastic in a sprinkle blend and are usually more detailed than a shaped sprinkle or quin.

Sanding Sugar

This is refined sugar that hasn't been ground as finely as regular granulated sugar. The larger crystals reflect light and give baked goods a shimmery appearance. Sanding sugar can be purchased in every color of the rainbow, but it's also very simple to tint your own (see page 15).

Sugar Crystals

AKA: *Coarse Sugar; Crystal Sugar; Decorating Sugar; Sparkling Sugar; Coarse Sanding Sugar*

Some may say that sugar crystals fall under the category of sanding sugar, since they are essentially the same thing. However, I feel it's important to make a distinction between the two. A sugar crystal grain is much larger and more rectangular in shape than a grain of sanding sugar. Sugar crystals are perfect for replicating tiny jewels, glass beads, or even aquarium rocks.

Rock Candy

AKA: *Rock Sugar*

These very large chunks of sugar crystals are usually sold still attached to the string or stick on which they were formed. Rock candy is way more difficult to chew than sanding sugar or sugar crystals, but it's just *so pretty*! I recommend removing really large pieces before digging into your trendy geode cake, or be sure to have your dentist on speed dial.

Pearl Sugar

AKA: *Nib Sugar; Hail Sugar*

Not to be confused with sugar pearls, pearl sugar is small, irregularly-shaped, rounded chunks of sugar. It can be added to a batter before baking for an element of crunch, or used to top pastries before they go into the oven.

Candy Shreds

AKA: *Wafer Shreds*

Candy shreds are short, thin strands of edible wafer paper that come in a variety of colors. They look like long classic sprinkles, but they're light as a feather. Wafer paper dissolves easily when it comes into contact with moisture, so add shreds to a buttercream-iced cake shortly before serving. See some on page 4!

Edible Glitter

AKA: *Glitter Shapes; Cake Sparkles*

Made from a combination of gelatin and food coloring, edible glitter shimmers and shines just like the real thing. It's available in a wide variety of shapes and sizes including fine glitter, chunky flakes, stars, hearts, butterflies, sequins, and more. Check it out on Lucky Star Cake (page 186)!

FOOD COLORING GUIDE

Water-Based Food Coloring

Found at the supermarket in little squeeze-y bottles with pointy lids, water-based food coloring makes it difficult to achieve deep, bold colors. And because it's water-based, it can thin out frostings or cake batters.

Gel Food Coloring

Thick, deep, and concentrated, gel coloring can be found at craft stores, big box stores, online, and even in some supermarkets. It comes in a wide variety of colors and is ideal for tinting cake batter, cookie dough, and buttercream. Gel coloring won't thin out your batter or bleed out of frostings.

Food Coloring Spray

AKA: *Color Mist*

This is happiness in a can, if you ask me! Spray food colorings are available in a limited number of solid colors and metallics. They're best used to cover a surface with a thin, opaque coat of color. I keep pearl shimmer spray in my purse at all times. It makes everything prettier.

gel

water-based

natural

oil-based

cocoa
butter

spray

metallic highlighter

disco dust

petal dust

powdered

Food Color Markers

Markers are perfect for adding small details that would otherwise need to be piped (no, thank you), like dots in eyes or flower stamens. They're great to have around to add a quick message to a cookie or chocolate plaque.

Oil-Based Food Coloring

AKA: *Candy Food Coloring*

Oil-based food coloring is designed to tint coating chocolate and white chocolate. Water-based colors would cause chocolate to seize or become thick and unusable.

Colored Cocoa Butter

Using colored cocoa butter is the best way to tint and add detail to chocolate work. These butters are still something of a specialty item, so you'll most likely have to purchase them online, unless you live in a major city with a high-end chef's market. Colored cocoa butters last quite a while, and a little goes a long way.

Powdered Food Coloring

Powdered food coloring provides another way to add color to mediums with a high fat content, like chocolate and coating chocolate. It's also great to use in addition to gel food coloring when tinting buttercream in deep, concentrated shades like bright red or purple.

Petal Dust

A colored powder used for adding detail and shading to finished decorations, petal dust is primarily used to add depth to flower petals in sugar-flower making. Petal dust can be brushed on dry to create a smoky effect, or mixed with a clear extract or grain alcohol and used like a paint. The extract or alcohol quickly evaporates, leaving just the color behind. Petal dust can be found at craft stores and on cake decorating websites.

Luster Dust

AKA: *Pearl Dust*

Luster dust provides an edible way to add a little shimmer and shine to your cake creations. Look for luster dusts that have been FDA-approved for food use. You can find a small assortment in most craft stores and a wide array on cake decorating websites. Like petal dust, luster dust can be brushed on dry or mixed with a clear extract or grain alcohol and used as a paint.

Disco Dust

AKA: *Twinkle Dust; Mystical Dust*

Disco dust is a chunkier version of luster dust, similar to glitter. Many varieties of disco dust are not considered food-safe, so look for ones labeled as FDA-approved.

Metallic Highlighter

Metallic highlighter is sold at cake supply stores and online. It is not edible and is designed only to be used on decorations that will be removed before serving. When mixed with a clear extract or grain alcohol, it creates a paint that leaves behind a dramatic, solid, and metallic finish.

Natural Food Coloring

Until recently, if you wanted to color cake batters or frostings naturally, you'd have to make your own food coloring by cooking down various fruits and vegetables. There are now a number of natural and even organic food colorings available online and in health food stores. Trucolor makes exceptionally bright all-natural food colorings. Store-bought natural food dyes can be a little pricier than traditional food coloring, but they're far easier than DIY-ing and provide more consistent coloring since they're produced on a large scale. Adding homemade natural food dyes may also alter the flavor of your finished product, so try to pair natural-colored ingredients with the flavor of cake or frosting you're making. Use homemade food dyes shortly after making them. Without preservatives, natural color will fade over time.

RED AND PINK: Canned beet juice or the strained puree from any red fruit (berries, pomegranates, cranberries)

ORANGE: Carrot juice

YELLOW: Turmeric or a small amount of carrot juice

GREEN: Spinach juice or liquid chlorophyll (available at health food stores)

BLUE: Boil red cabbage in a small amount of water. The water will turn blue. Or use blueberry or blackberry juice.

PURPLE: Add a small amount of baking soda to the blue cabbage water to turn it purple, or use blackberry or blueberry juice.

COLORING YOUR OWN
sprinkles and sanding sugar

» Pour sprinkles or sanding sugar into a zip-top bag.

» Dip a toothpick into gel food coloring and smear a tiny dot on the inside of the bag. Start with a very small amount of coloring and add more until you achieve your desired shade.

» Seal the bag and shake to coat the sprinkles or sanding sugar.

» Pour the sprinkles or sanding sugar onto a parchment-lined cookie sheet. Allow the sprinkles or sanding sugar to dry out, at least 30 minutes or up to overnight, before storing.

UNICORN thought

Chapter 2

....

THE KNOW-HOW

CAKE ANATOMY

I AM GOING TO TELL YOU A SECRET ABOUT CAKE RECIPES:
They're all the same. Well, that's not to say that all cake recipes are
created equal, but they do all share similar ratios of ingredients that add
tenderness, strength, and flavor. Otherwise, they wouldn't work. Add a
little too much or not enough of something, and the recipe will fail in any
number of ways—too dense, too dry, too soupy, etc. Creating a foolproof
cake recipe isn't sorcery, it's science.

Some ingredients fall into more than one category, but all perform
at least one of those three main tasks. In math, the values on either side
of the equal sign need to be the same for the equation to be correct. In
a recipe—or more accurately, a formula—the ingredients in all three categories need to balance one another out in order to bake a delicious cake.

Strength ✚ *Tenderness* ✚ *Flavor* ⊜ *Cake Heaven*

Strength

» *Flour, egg whites, whole eggs, water, milk, buttermilk*

Protein isn't just for studly beefcakes looking to bulk up—it's also a necessary component in traditional cake recipes. Flour contains gluten. (My gluten-free friends can see page 23 for more info.) Gluten is made of protein strands. When liquid is added to flour, the gluten gets to work. The protein strands wiggle around, grow bigger, and create the structure that all the other ingredients will live within. The protein in whole eggs and egg whites adds to that structure. The more you agitate gluten, the stronger it gets and the tougher your end product will be. The trick with making a tender cake is coaxing out just enough gluten to provide structure without making the cake tough and dry. So, when I say don't overmix, I mean it. Keep those glutens in check.

Liquids. I know. You're like, hold the phone! Liquids aren't strong. They're, uhhh . . . liquidy! How the heck do they add strength to a cake recipe?!? Truth is, they actually add both. Flour wouldn't be able to create its magical glutinous structure without the addition of a liquid. Milk is Mr. Complex, contributing both sugar and protein content to a recipe. If milk is Mr. Complex, then buttermilk is Queen of Complex-ia, contributing protein, sugar, and acidity to a recipe. All help to smooth out a batter and allow ingredients to more easily combine. Liquids are the multitasking unifiers of the cake world.

Tenderness

» *Butter, oil, sugar, egg yolks, acid, leaveners, milk*

Let's talk about the word *moist*. I know you've used it to describe a cake. I'm sure if you

polled people and asked them what qualities they look for in a delicious cake, *moist* would come up 100 out of 100 times. The trouble with the word *moist* is that it A) makes me cringe; and B) doesn't do good cake justice. It's not *technically* a correct way to describe a cake that is soft, delicate, and easy to chew. The word you're looking for is *tender*.

Doesn't *tender* automatically make you feel better? I hear *moist* and I think of dirty sponges and New Jersey. I hear *tender* and think of little white cuddly bears, surrounded by hearts and bouncing on dryer sheets. Now you just need to convince all of your friends and family to stop using the word *moist* and hop on the *tender* train. The world will be a better place for it.

Fats and sweeteners (or anything with sugar in it, like milk) are the main contributors to a cake's tender goodness. Both are also major players in the flavor category. They work their magic by being little troublemakers. Fats and sweeteners wreak havoc in your mixing bowl by breaking down some of that beautiful structure the strengtheners work so hard to create. Leaveners are like covert ops. They sneak into the open links of gluten's protein chains, release gas bubbles, and then *POP* the bubbles during the baking process. Their shenanigans leave the gluten structure rattled, but not entirely destroyed. It's an epic battle that, when executed correctly, results in a soft, light-as-air cake with a delicate, fine crumb.

Flavor

» *Salt, extracts, spices*

What good is it to create a perfectly balanced cake recipe if it doesn't *taste* like magic? Extracts and spices are typically added in such small amounts that there's no

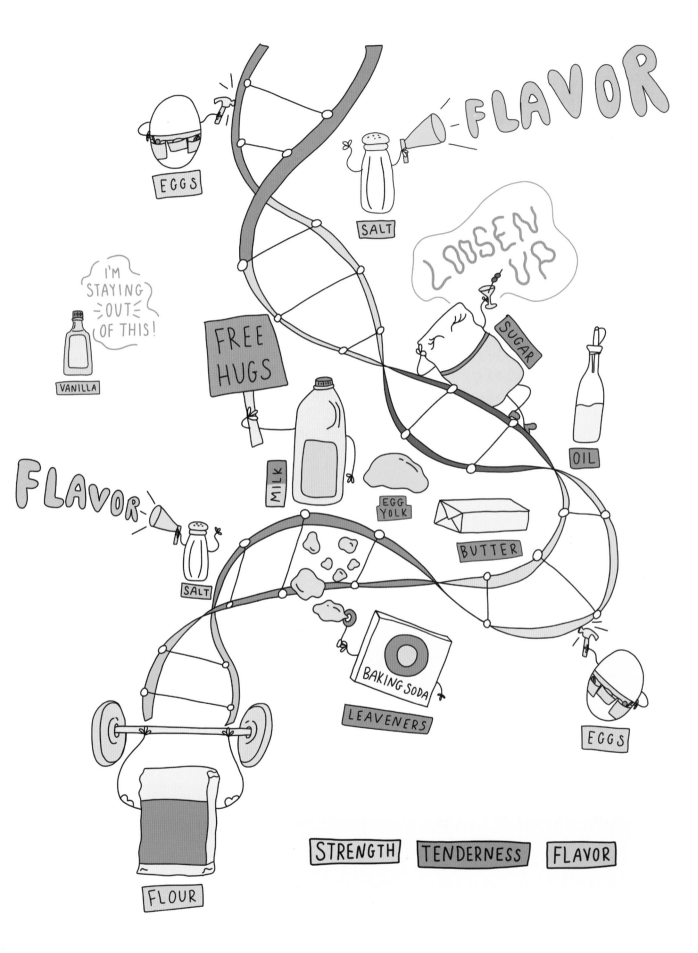

BAKING FAUX REAL

I've dedicated most of my adult life and part of my childhood to developing exceptional recipes for cakes, buttercreams, fillings, cookies, and more. But even I am not above busting open a box of cake mix from time to time. The bake sale cupcakes can be works of art next time. It's 9 p.m. and Momma's got some *Real Housewives* to catch up on. Nights like those, use these tips and tricks to turn mixes and store-bought ingredients into cake masterpieces that'll leave them wondering where you found the time.

Cake

» To mimic the flavor and density of vanilla cake that's been baked from scratch, add one extra-large egg yolk and a 3.5-ounce box of instant vanilla pudding mix to a box of vanilla or yellow cake mix, along with the rest of the ingredients called for on the cake mix box. No need to make the pudding—just dump in the powdered mix.

» For chocolate cake, do the same to a chocolate or devil's food cake mix, but use chocolate instant pudding mix.

» Create cake flavor variations by changing up the flavor of the pudding mix you add to the cake mix. Add complementing extracts to further enhance the flavor.

Filling and Frosting

» Create a thick, custardy filling by making a 3.5-ounce box of instant pudding with half as much milk as called for on the box. For an even richer custard, substitute heavy cream for the milk.

» Use store-bought jam as a filling on its own or use it to flavor canned frosting or jarred lemon curd.

» Make a faux mousse by whipping 1 quart of heavy cream with a 3.5-ounce box of instant pudding mix. Go even more faux and create a similar filling by whisking a box of instant pudding mix into an 8-ounce tub of whipped topping.

» Raid the sundae aisle for cake fixings. Caramel sundae topping can be used as a filling on its own or to flavor canned frosting.

» Lighten and flavor a traditional American buttercream (page 57) by adding a 3.5-ounce box of instant pudding mix to the butter as it's whipping.

» Create a quick, pourable glaze by scooping a can of frosting into a heatproof bowl. Microwave until it's thin and runny (15 to 20 seconds).

need to provide balance in other parts of the cake formula. The exception to that rule is when a flavor adds acidity. In that case, the leavener would likely need to be adjusted.

Salt should become your new best friend. Adding salt to your cake recipe doesn't make it taste salty. It takes your cakes from good to great. Each little granule is like a tiny megaphone, amplifying the flavors around it.

Measuring

If you're going the extra mile to bake from scratch, then you might as well take a few seconds to measure properly. Always, *always* use dry measures for dry and wet measures for wet to ensure your recipe bakes up as desired. The delicate balance of ingredients outlined above depends upon you treating each of them in a specific way. This goes not just for my recipes, but for cake recipes across the board.

FLOUR: Most books say to spoon flour into your measuring cup to prevent it from becoming too densely packed. Both you and I know you won't be opening the spoon drawer anytime soon, so simply use your measuring cup to fluff the flour before scooping and leveling the top with the back edge of a knife or icing spatula.

SMALL DRY INGREDIENTS (BAKING SODA, BAKING POWDER, SPICES): Fluff, scoop, and level just like measuring flour.

BUTTER: Use the marks on the wrapper as your guide. Measure butter before melting it, unless specified otherwise.

LIQUIDS: Place your liquid measuring cup on a flat surface before pouring in any liquids. Bend over (don't lift the cup up) to make sure you've hit the mark.

BROWN SUGAR: Use the palm of your hand to tightly pack brown sugar into the proper measuring cup. Level the top with the back edge of a knife or icing spatula.

MAKE NOW, BAKE LATER

Baker, meet your new best friend—the freezer. Here's a baking secret most pros know and love: You don't need to make and bake at the same time. Make doughs or batters when you have the time, then freeze them for later use. A teeny bit of planning will make your life a whole lot easier the night before the bake sale or a big holiday party.

You'll notice that I specifically freeze batters and doughs. I know some people swear by freezing finished cakes and cookies, but I'm just not a fan. The freezing and thawing process causes liquids to contract and expand, leaving the finished baked good just kind of OK. Nowhere near the heaven that is hot cookies or warm cake straight from the oven.

Freezing Cake Batter

Not all cake batters can be frozen. Freezing and thawing chiffon or sponge-style batters (leavened with whipped egg whites, like Vanilla Birthday Cake) will ruin the batter. Creaming-method cake batters (Chocolate Birthday Cake, the "Any" recipes) freeze beautifully. Most batters and doughs can be stored in the freezer for up to 3 months.

» Store small portions (for cupcakes and mini cakes) in single-serving reusable freezer containers. Use dishers or portion scoops to divide the batter equally among the containers. Leave a ½ inch or so of space at the top to allow for the batter to expand and contract during the freezing and thawing process.

» Store larger amounts of cake batter in zip-top freezer bags, smooshing all of the air out first so that the bag lays flat in the freezer.

» Put the cake batter in the fridge to defrost the night before you want to use it. Give the batter a stir and portion into prepared cake pans. Bake according to your recipe.

» Defrosted cake batter straight from the fridge will have a tighter crumb than cake batter that comes to room temperature before baking.

Freezing Cookie Doughs

Similar to cake batters (see previous page), cookie doughs that employ egg whites in any way (meringues, tuiles) will not freeze well. Creamed doughs (sugar cookie, drop, shortbread, etc.) freeze perfectly.

SUGAR COOKIES

» Store batches of sugar cookie dough in the freezer, wrapped in plastic wrap and sealed in a zip-top bag, for up to 3 months. Thaw in the fridge overnight before using.

» Roll sugar cookie dough between two pieces of parchment paper and store on a cookie sheet in the fridge until needed. Stack rolled sheets on top of one another on the same cookie sheet. Wrap the cookie sheet with plastic wrap and store it in the freezer for up to 3 months. Pull individual sheets from the freezer as needed. Cut and bake cookies straight from the freezer.

» Roll and cut cookie shapes. Place them on a lined cookie sheet and into the freezer until frozen solid, about 30 minutes. Layer the shapes between pieces of parchment paper in an airtight container. Freeze for up to 3 months. Pull cookie shapes right from the freezer and bake according to the recipe's instructions.

DROP COOKIES

» Use a disher to scoop uniform rounds of cookie dough onto a lined cookie sheet. Pop the sheet in the freezer until the dough is frozen solid. Gather up the frozen cookie dough balls and store in a large zip-top freezer bag. Freezing them on the sheet prevents the cookies from hardening into a giant ball of dough and allows you to pull single cookies as needed (or wanted).

» Some cookie doughs bake perfectly straight from the freezer. Others work better if thawed first. Test a cookie or two with your own recipe.

LOVE ALL, BAKE ALL

I'm guessing you know at least one person with a dietary restriction of some kind—gluten free, dairy free, soy free, vegan, no refined sugar, tree nut allergy, egg allergy, casein allergy, and so on. It can be overwhelming—and even worse, isolating—for the person suffering from the allergy or restriction. With cake being the most important celebratory food in our culture (sorry, salad), not being able to partake in the party time can be downright depressing.

Right before I opened my bakery, my sister was diagnosed with celiac disease, my father shortly thereafter. Luckily, I dodged the genetic bullet and can still indulge in my favorite glutenous treats. After their diagnoses, I went on a cake odyssey, determined to find a way to make tasty treats my entire family could enjoy. While on this journey, and in my time baking a zillion wedding cakes for the population at large, I ran into every other allergy and food restriction under the sun. And, I dare say, I conquered most. Here are my findings.

Flour

If you solely need to eliminate gluten from your recipe, don't mess with a good thing. Just pick up the best gluten-free flour blend you can find and follow their replacement suggestions. Gluten-free flour blends have come leaps and bounds since I first tried baking a gluten-free cake. I've gone through endless experiments attempting to create my own blend and in the end, the ready-made ones are tough to beat. King Arthur Flour and Cup4Cup are two of my favorite brands. As with anything, read through their ingredients before purchasing to make sure the flour blend works with your specific restriction.

Gluten and grains are a more complex subject for some. Rice, potato, and corn provide starchiness to most commercially produced gluten-free flour blends. My rule of thumb when I need to create a custom GF flour blend is equal parts GF grain to GF starch. If none of the grains work for you, then combine equal parts of two starches. When creating your own GF flour blend, it is helpful, but not 100-percent necessary, to add a small amount of xanthan gum (about ½ teaspoon) for added structure and stability.

GLUTEN-FREE GRAIN FLOURS	GLUTEN-FREE STARCHES
Brown rice flour	Potato starch
Millet flour	Cornstarch
Corn flour	Arrowroot flour
Sorghum flour	White rice flour
Oat flour	Tapioca flour

Eggs

My favorite substitute for whole eggs in a cake recipe is Ener-G egg replacer. It can be found in most health food stores, some supermarkets, and online. Their egg replacer is made with a combination of starches that replace some of the structure eggs provide without adding an unpleasant flavor or texture.

If you can't do starches, my second favorite egg replacer is flaxseed meal. (No need to break out the coffee grinder; most health food stores and some supermarkets sell flaxseeds already ground.) Combine 1 tablespoon ground flaxseed with 3 tablespoons water. Set the mixture aside for at least 5 minutes to thicken. Flax eggs can add a touch of nutty flavor to a cake recipe. They're best used in cakes where the added flavor will be masked, like a chocolate cake or carrot cake.

Most egg replacers work best in recipes where the egg is used whole. In chiffon-style recipes, where the egg whites are whipped and used as a leavener, the best solution is bean juice. Yup. Keep reading for more on this.

Egg Whites

You read that right: bean juice. Aquafaba, or the run-off juices from a can of chickpeas, recently set the egg-free-baking world ablaze. No one is really all that sure why chickpea juice produces an uncanny whipped egg white substitution. Other bean juices work as well, but I prefer chickpea because it's clear and relatively tasteless (and I really like hummus). Whip up 2 tablespoons aquafaba for every egg white called for in your recipe. Literally just use the liquid straight from the can. Magic.

Vegetable Oil

In most cake recipes (and when making box mixes), vegetable oil can be easily replaced with whatever oil you have on hand. Light olive oil works well, as does coconut oil. Be sure to measure the coconut oil after you've melted it, not before.

Milk

In the majority of cake recipes, milk can simply be replaced with water. You'll lose a teensy bit of fat and sugar, but it's so small that it's hardly missed. In addition, most supermarkets now carry a large selection of diary-free milk substitutes. If you already have

Friends don't make other friends sick (or at least they try their best not to). If baking for someone with a food restriction makes you nervous, go faux and buy a box mix. It's a safe, easy, and effective way to make something you can be sure of. It's also cost effective, since you'll need to break open new ingredients (bag of sugar, stick of butter, etc.) to ensure they haven't been tainted by allergens.

UNICORN thought

soy or almond milk in your kitchen, by all means use it. Just be sure to buy the plain varieties without any added sugar or flavoring.

Buttermilk

Ah, good old Queen of Complex-ia. Replacing this multifaceted ingredient is actually pretty easy. Combine 1 cup milk or nondairy milk with 1 tablespoon white vinegar or lemon juice. Set the mixture aside for at least 5 minutes before using to allow the mixture to curdle. Or, replace buttermilk with the same amount of nondairy sour cream or yogurt.

Refined Sugar

Coconut sugar is a terrific one-to-one replacement for refined white sugar in most cake recipes. Its flavor is more similar to brown sugar, but it's dry and granulated like regular white sugar. My local supermarkets all carry coconut sugar now, making it easier to bake for my refined-sugar-free friends. You can also find it at health food stores and online.

There are many liquid replacements for refined sugar—maple syrup, molasses, and honey, to name a few—but they are very difficult to substitute one-to-one in most cake recipes without significantly changing the cake's flavor and texture. If you're adept at adjusting recipes, or have eliminated refined sugars for life, then go for it! If you're simply trying to throw together a quick dessert that all of your friends can enjoy, spring for the coconut sugar.

Butter

Replacing butter breaks my heart, but I know for some it must be done. If dairy is your sole concern, butter can be replaced one-to-one with shortening in both cake and frosting recipes. Most supermarkets also now carry at least one, if not more, vegan butter substitute. Earth's Balance is a widely available brand that has worked well for me in cake recipes, but I do prefer shortening over vegan butter when making dairy-free frostings. Coconut oil is another good substitute in cake recipes. Just be sure to measure it in its solid form when using as a butter replacer.

CALL IN THE SUBS -

It's 10 p.m. on Sunday night and everything is closed. The butter's softened, the chocolate's melted, and you've just poured yourself a glass of wine when you realize you're short an ingredient. Pull a cake-MacGyver and make do with what you have.

INGREDIENT	SUBSTITUTION
Buttermilk, 1 cup	1 tablespoon acid (lemon juice, vinegar) plus 1 cup milk (dairy or nondairy); or 1 cup plain yogurt or sour cream
Cake flour, 1 cup	2 tablespoons cornstarch plus enough all-purpose flour to equal 1 cup
Baking powder, 1 teaspoon	¼ teaspoon baking soda, ¼ teaspoon cornstarch, and ½ teaspoon cream of tartar
Sour cream, 1 cup	1 cup yogurt
Brown sugar, 1 cup	1 cup granulated sugar plus 2 tablespoons molasses
Kosher salt, 1 teaspoon	¾ teaspoon table salt
Dutch-processed cocoa powder, 1 cup	1 cup unsweetened or natural cocoa powder plus ¾ teaspoon baking soda

PART 2
piece of cake

Chapter 3

·····································

CAKE

I'M ~~A LAZY~~ AN EFFICIENT BAKER. I TREASURE TOOLS AND ingredients that perform multiple tasks. Over the years I've honed and tweaked these recipes, squeezing every last ounce of usefulness out of them. The similarities between working in a professional kitchen and in my home kitchen with two small children running around are striking. In both settings, it's loud, people are yelling at me, they need their food now, now, *now,* and someone's taking their pants off behind the counter. The efficiency of these recipes is as useful in a chaotic restaurant kitchen as it is in a busy home.

Things you may notice about my cake recipes . . .

» I add all the small measurement ingredients (baking soda, baking powder, salt, extracts, etc.) in with the butter and sugar when making a batter using the creaming method. I started doing this at the bakery when I'd be in the kitchen prepping batters, answering phones, and dealing with customers all by my lonesome. I knew if I put all the small ingredients in with the butter, I'd only have the flour left to add as a dry ingredient if I got pulled away from my prep. Good luck figuring out if you've added the baking powder in with the flour after walking away from it for an hour. Adding these small ingredients in this step also helps them to incorporate better throughout the batter.

» I don't sift anything, because I don't want to. I wasn't lying when I said I am . . . efficient. Adding the small ingredients in with the butter eliminates the need for this step in most recipes.

» Recipe yield is provided in cups, in addition to cake size. I don't know how you fill your pans at home and you don't know how I fill my pans at home, so let's stop pretending that any of us really knows what "Makes two 8-inch round cakes" means. It's especially frustrating when you want to adapt a recipe to make larger or smaller cakes. Knowing how many cups a batter yields will allow you to make better decisions regarding how much batter you make and what you bake it in. Reference the chart on page 222 to see how many cups of batter you need for the size cake you want to make.

» The cake recipes in this book all yield two tall 8-inch round cakes or three regular 6-inch round cakes. Use the tall 8-inch cakes as-is with a single layer of filling or split them to create four layers of cake with three layers of filling, like in the pictured Cakequations. I'm a frosting gal myself, so I like a cake filled with lots of creamy goodness. If you prefer more cake than frosting, skip the slicing and extra filling.

» Cakes are cooled in the pan and then on a flat surface, like a plate or clean countertop. Hot pans can be placed on a trivet, dish towel, or pot holder. Cooling cakes directly on a rack leaves marks on their beautiful, flat bottoms. Keeping the bottoms of the cakes smooth makes them a little easier to crumb coat and finish. It also prevents softer cakes from tearing or becoming indented on the cooling rack.

» *Any* actually means *any-ish*. I'm really looking forward to my first well-intentioned I-told-you-so e-mail. I apologize in advance if the Any Fruit Cake recipe doesn't work with the durian fruit that you brought back from Thailand. I didn't get around to testing that fruit. Please do try these recipes with whatever ideas you may have of your own. Just keep in mind that the variations listed are the ones that I know work, and work well. Puree durian at your own risk.

» They are delicious.

FOAMING METHOD
AKA: Sponge, genoise, or egg foam method

When putting together a cake recipe that employs the foaming method, you have to whip it. Whip it good. The eggs, that is! First, air is beaten into the eggs—whole (genoise) or whites only (sponge). Next, granulated sugar is added to the eggs while they're whipping, providing a place for water to hide in the mixing process. After the dry ingredients have been combined with the wet, avoid deflating the eggs by folding them in ever so gently. When you apply heat, some of the water in the batter will evaporate, leaving behind a beautiful, aerated egg protein structure. Be sure to use a clean, dry bowl and tools when whipping your eggs. The presence of any contaminant, especially fats, will prevent your whites (and subsequently, your cake) from reaching its fluffy potential.

» Vanilla Birthday Cake

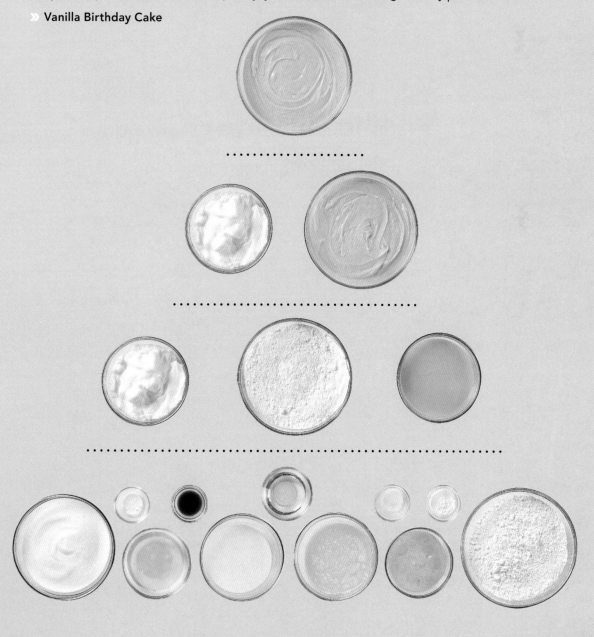

Yields:

» *10 cups batter*
» *Two tall 8-inch round cakes*
» *Three regular 6-inch round cakes*

5 cups cake flour (plus more cake flour or all-purpose flour for the pans)

2½ teaspoons baking powder

½ teaspoon baking soda

1½ teaspoons kosher salt

12 large egg yolks

3½ cups granulated sugar

10 ounces unsalted butter, melted

6 tablespoons vegetable oil

4 teaspoons pure vanilla extract

1 cup buttermilk

6 large egg whites

BIRTHDAY CAKE

Go, shorty. It's your birthday. We're gonna party like it's your birthday. We're gonna bake cake for you like it's your birthday. And you know, we don't even care it's not your birthday!

    You can find me in the kitchen . . . OK, I'll stop. But seriously, don't wait until your birthday to make either version of this cake. These are my go-to, tried-and-true vanilla and chocolate cake recipes. They were the base cakes at my bakery. Most of the flavors we offered started with one of these recipes. I've included a number of variations for each, but consider them a starting point. I invite you to make these recipes your own and experiment with different flavor variation ideas.

Vanilla Birthday Cake

➕ **DOCTOR, DOCTOR!** *The boxed equivalent to this recipe would be a yellow cake or vanilla cake mix. For a denser cake that more closely resembles homemade, add 1 large egg yolk and one 3.5-ounce box of instant vanilla pudding mix to the ingredients called for on the box.*

//

1. Position a rack in the center of the oven and preheat to 350°F. Spray and flour pans in your chosen size.

2. In a large bowl, whisk together the flour, baking powder, baking soda, and salt.

3. In a medium bowl, whisk together the egg yolks, 2½ cups of the sugar, the melted butter, vegetable oil, and vanilla extract. Whisk in the buttermilk once the other ingredients have been combined so that it doesn't cause the melted butter to clump.

4. In the bowl of a stand mixer fitted with the whisk attachment (or in a large bowl using an electric hand mixer or an old-fashioned hand whisk), beat the egg whites on medium-high speed until stiff peaks form, 2 to 3 minutes. Turn the mixer to low speed and slowly add in the remaining 1 cup sugar. Return the mixer to high speed and whip the egg white mixture until stiff peaks form, another 2 to 3 minutes.

5. Pour the buttermilk mixture into the dry ingredients and whisk until combined.

6. Switch to a rubber spatula and gently fold the egg whites into the cake batter in three batches. Stir the first batch into the batter to loosen it up, but fold more delicately with the second and third batches. Take care not to deflate the egg whites or overmix the batter.

7. Divide the batter evenly between the prepared pans and bake, rotating the pans' positions halfway through baking, until a toothpick inserted in the center of a cake comes out clean or with a few crumbs clinging to it, 45 to 50 minutes for 8-inch round pans or 30 to 35 minutes for 6-inch round pans.

8. Transfer the cakes to a rack to cool in the pans for about 30 minutes. Turn the cakes out onto a flat surface, like plates or a clean countertop. Let the cakes cool completely before frosting, filling, or storing.

SEE IT IN A SLICE: *page 131*

★ Plastic is not fantastic when whipping egg whites, as it can absorb fats over time. Use a metal or copper bowl for foaming success.

★ Save those extra egg whites to whip up some gorgeous meringue decorations (pages 175 and 177) or to add crunchy meringue bits to your cake layers (page 86).

★ Powdered buttermilk is a busy baker's best friend. Find it in the supermarket's baking aisle and store in the fridge after opening for up to 3 years—no joke. Mix the quantity you need when you need it.

UNICORN thought

VANILLA BIRTHDAY CAKE VARIATIONS - - - - - - - - - - - - - - -

Lemon Birthday Cake	Add the grated zest of one lemon to the wet ingredients in step 3.
Blueberry Lemon Birthday Cake	Add the grated zest of one lemon to the wet ingredients in step 3. Stir 1½ cups fresh or frozen (unthawed) blueberries into the batter in step 5, before folding in the egg whites.
Ginger Birthday Cake	Add 1½ teaspoons ground ginger and ¼ cup ginger preserves to the wet ingredients in step 3.
Coconut Birthday Cake	Reduce the buttermilk to ½ cup and add ½ cup cream of coconut to the wet ingredients in step 3. Stir 1 cup shredded sweetened coconut into the batter in step 5, before folding in the egg whites.
Espresso Birthday Cake	Add 2 tablespoons Medaglia d'Oro instant espresso powder to the buttermilk. Microwave for 1 minute, or warm in a small saucepan, to dissolve the powder.
Orange Clove Birthday Cake	Add the grated zest of one orange and 1 teaspoon ground cloves to the wet ingredients in step 3.
Almond Birthday Cake	Add 4 teaspoons almond extract to the wet ingredients in step 3.
Toffee Birthday Cake	Stir 1½ cups finely chopped toffee bits (page 81) into the batter in step 5, before folding in the egg whites.
Spice Birthday Cake	Add 1½ teaspoons ground cinnamon, 1 teaspoon ground ginger, ¼ teaspoon ground allspice, and ⅛ teaspoon ground cloves to the wet ingredients in step 3.
Funfetti Birthday Cake	Stir 1 cup rainbow confetti quins or sprinkles into the batter in step 5, before folding in the egg whites.
Chocolate Chip Birthday Cake	Stir 1 cup mini chocolate chips into the batter in step 5, before folding in the egg whites.

CREAMING METHOD

AKA: Two-bowl, dump, muffin, or all-ingredient method

The creaming method is what's used most frequently in American cake recipes. The fat (typically butter) is aerated by beating it together with sugar. Tiny ninja-like sugar crystals slice and dice their way through the dense fat, creating pockets of air that work together with the leavening agent to give the finished cake a light, airy texture. Time and temperature are the keys to creaming perfection. Room-temperature butter allows the sugar to do its job properly. Butter that is too warm (runny or melted) won't allow any air pockets to form. Butter that's too cold won't give enough when the sugar tries to cut through. Over-creaming the butter creates too many air pockets, causing the structure of the cake to collapse when baking. Properly creamed butter will be fluffy and light in color, with barely any sugar grit left to it.

» **Chocolate Birthday Cake**

» **Any Butter Cake**

» **Any Pound Cake**

Black Velvet
variation
(page 38)

Chocolate Birthday Cake

➕ **DOCTOR, DOCTOR!** *The boxed equivalent to this recipe would be a devil's food or dark chocolate cake mix. For a denser cake that more closely resembles homemade, add 1 large egg yolk and one 3.5-ounce box of instant chocolate pudding mix to the ingredients called for on the box.*

///

1. Position a rack in the center of the oven and preheat to 350°F. Spray and flour pans in your chosen size.

2. In the bowl of a stand mixer fitted with the paddle attachment (or in a large bowl using an electric hand mixer), beat together the butter, brown sugar, granulated sugar, baking soda, and salt at medium speed until fluffy and lighter in color, stopping to scrape down the sides of the bowl with a rubber spatula to make sure there are no butter lumps, about 5 minutes.

3. Add the eggs, one at a time, until completely combined. Stop and scrape down the sides of the bowl halfway through mixing and after adding the last egg.

4. In a medium bowl, whisk together the cocoa powder and warm water until combined. Once the cocoa powder has dissolved, add the milk and whisk to combine.

5. With the mixer on low, add half of the flour to the butter mixture until just incorporated. Slowly add half of the milk mixture until combined. Stop and scrape down the sides of the bowl with a rubber spatula. Add the remaining flour and mix until just incorporated. Add the last of the wet ingredients and mix until combined.

6. Divide the batter evenly between the prepared pans and bake, rotating the pans' positions halfway through baking, until a toothpick inserted in the center of a cake comes out clean or with a few crumbs clinging to it, 45 to 50 minutes for 8-inch round pans or 30 to 35 minutes for 6-inch round pans.

➡️

Yields:
- 10 cups batter
- Two tall 8-inch round cakes
- Three regular 6-inch round cakes

8 ounces unsalted butter, softened

2½ cups packed dark brown sugar

1½ cups granulated sugar

2 teaspoons baking soda

2 teaspoons kosher salt

8 large eggs

1½ cups Dutch-processed cocoa powder

2 cups warm water

1 cup whole milk

4 cups all-purpose flour (plus more for the pans)

**SEE IT IN
A SLICE:**
page 157

7. Transfer the cakes to a rack to cool in the pan for about
30 minutes. Turn the cakes out onto a flat surface, like plates or a
clean countertop. Let the cakes cool completely before frosting,
filling, or storing.

CHOCOLATE BIRTHDAY CAKE VARIATIONS ----------------

Mocha Birthday Cake	Add ¼ cup Medaglia d'Oro instant espresso powder to the cocoa powder and warm water in step 4.
Red Velvet Birthday Cake	Reduce the cocoa powder to ¾ cup and add 2 tablespoons red food coloring to the cocoa powder and warm water in step 4.
Black Velvet Birthday Cake	Substitute black cocoa powder (cocoa noir) for the Dutch-processed cocoa powder.
Chocolate Toffee Birthday Cake	Stir 1½ cups finely chopped toffee bits into the finished batter in step 5.
Double Chocolate Birthday Cake	Stir 1½ cups mini chocolate chips into the finished batter in step 5.

Any Butter Cake

The butter I'm referring to in this recipe doesn't come from a cow, but rather from grinding seeds, nuts, or even cookies to a smooth paste. To keep the recipe balanced, try to purchase butters with as few additional ingredients as possible. It is entirely up to you whether you use a nut or seed butter that's been left chunky, or one that's been ground completely smooth. Butters with added sugar (like my dear love, Nutella) can be used if you reduce the amount of sugar indicated in the main recipe (see the chart on the next page for details).

It's difficult not to start every recipe by saying, "This is my favorite cake." I love all my babies equally, for different reasons. But this is my favorite cake. It just is. I apologize to the others, but for me, this cake hits every spot—nutty, salty, buttery, sweet, tender, and still delicious on day three. It's perfectly wonderful on its own, but also plays nicely with others (like chocolate ganache or raspberry jam). Make it with sunflower seed butter and you'll be crowned queen of the allergy-friendly bake sale. Whip up the hazelnut variation and you'll leave the ladies at book club speechless. The Nutella version? Just stop. It's almost too much of a good thing. Almost.

Yields:
- » *10 cups batter*
- » *Two tall 8-inch round cakes*
- » *Three regular 6-inch round cakes*

12 ounces unsalted butter, softened

Ground butter (see chart)

Granulated sugar (see chart)

2 teaspoons pure vanilla extract

1 tablespoon baking powder

1 teaspoon kosher salt

9 large eggs

1½ cups cake flour (plus more cake flour or all-purpose flour for the pans)

---

1. Position a rack in the center of the oven and preheat to 350°F. Spray and flour pans in your chosen size.

2. In the bowl of a stand mixer fitted with the paddle attachment (or in a large bowl using an electric hand mixer), beat together the unsalted butter, ground butter, granulated sugar, vanilla extract, baking powder, and salt at medium speed until fluffy and lighter in

When measuring sticky ingredients, like ground butters, grease the cup first with a light coating of shortening, butter, or cooking spray. The measured amount will slide right out, leaving you with an easy cleanup.

UNICORN thought

**SEE IT IN
A SLICE:**
page 134

color, stopping to scrape down the sides of the bowl with a rubber spatula to make sure there are no butter lumps, about 5 minutes.

3. Add the eggs, one at a time, until completely combined. Stop and scrape down the sides of the bowl halfway through mixing and after adding the last egg.

4. With the mixer on low, slowly add the flour to the butter mixture until just incorporated. Scrape down the sides of the bowl one last time. Fold in any remaining streaks of flour by hand.

5. Divide the batter evenly between the prepared pans and bake, rotating the pans' positions halfway through baking, until a toothpick inserted in the center of a cake comes out clean or with a few crumbs clinging to it, 45 to 50 minutes for 8-inch round pans or 30 to 35 minutes for 6-inch round pans.

6. Transfer the cakes to a rack to cool in the pan for about 30 minutes. Turn the cakes out onto a flat surface, like plates or a clean countertop. Let the cakes cool completely before frosting, filling, or storing.

BUTTER CAKE VARIATIONS ----------------------

	GROUND BUTTER	**GRANULATED SUGAR**
Cashew Butter Cake	12 ounces cashew butter	1¾ cups
Peanut Butter Cake	12 ounces peanut butter	1¾ cups
Almond Butter Cake	12 ounces almond butter	1¾ cups
Nutella Cake	12 ounces Nutella	¾ cup
Cookie Butter Cake	12 ounces cookie butter	¾ cup
Hazelnut Butter Cake	12 ounces hazelnut paste	1¾ cups
Sun Butter Cake	12 ounces sunflower seed butter	1¾ cups

Any Pound Cake

Any pound cake's superpowers are derived from its ability to change dramatically by simply swapping a sweetener. This had exclusively been my go-to Honey Pound Cake recipe, until I started to wonder what more could be done with it. If honey works, what about maple syrup? (As any good New Englander would ask.) If those work, why am I still making a separate gingerbread cake recipe when I'm betting (and I guessed right) that molasses would work, too?

Pound cake is dense and rich. (Its counterpart in bizarro cake world would be angel food cake.) For that reason, it's best paired with fillings that are bright in flavor (think citrus or berry). Its soft but sturdy texture provides the perfect counterpoint to an added element of crunch in its layers. For simpler affairs, this cake stands on its own with a drizzle of jam or sugar glaze. It's coffee and tea's best friend.

//

1. Position a rack in the center of the oven and preheat to 350°F. Spray and flour pans in your chosen size.

2. In the bowl of a stand mixer fitted with the paddle attachment (or in a large bowl using an electric hand mixer), beat together the butter, sugar, baking powder, salt, vanilla extract, and optional spices at medium speed until fluffy and lighter in color, stopping to scrape down the sides of the bowl with a rubber spatula to make sure there are no butter lumps, about 5 minutes. Drizzle in the sweetener on low speed until just combined.

→

Yields:
» *10 cups batter*
» *Two tall 8-inch round cakes*
» *Three regular 6-inch round cakes*

20 ounces unsalted butter, softened

2 cups granulated sugar

4 teaspoons baking powder

1 teaspoon kosher salt

4 teaspoons pure vanilla extract

Spices (see chart)

Liquid sweetener (see chart)

8 large eggs

6 cups all-purpose flour (plus more for the pans)

2 cups whole milk

★ *When measuring sticky ingredients, like liquid sweeteners, grease the cup first with a light coating of shortening, butter, or cooking spray. The measured amount will slide right out, leaving you with an easy cleanup.*

★ *When buying maple syrup, leave the sweet little lady on the shelf and spring for the good stuff. Look for pure maple syrup that contains no added ingredients, not "pancake syrup."*

UNICORN thought

SEE IT IN A SLICE:
page 120

3. Add the eggs, one at a time, until completely combined. Stop and scrape down the sides of the bowl halfway through mixing and after adding the last egg.

4. With the mixer on low, add half of the flour to the butter mixture until just incorporated. Slowly add half of the milk until combined. Stop and scrape down the sides of the bowl with a rubber spatula. Add the remaining flour and mix until just incorporated. Add the last of the milk and mix until combined.

5. Divide the batter evenly between the prepared pans and bake, rotating the pans' positions halfway through baking, until a toothpick inserted in the center of a cake comes out clean or with a few crumbs clinging to it, 45 to 55 minutes for 8-inch round pans or 35 to 40 minutes for 6-inch round pans.

6. Transfer the cakes to a rack to cool in the pan for about 30 minutes. Turn the cakes out onto a flat surface, like plates or a clean countertop. Let the cakes cool completely before frosting, filling, or storing.

POUND CAKE VARIATIONS

	SPICES	LIQUID SWEETENER
Honey Pound Cake		12 ounces honey
Gingerbread Pound Cake	2 teaspoons ground cinnamon 1 teaspoon ground ginger ¼ teaspoon ground cloves Pinch finely ground black pepper	12 ounces molasses
Maple Pound Cake		12 ounces maple syrup

QUICK-MIX METHOD
AKA: Two-bowl, dump, muffin, or all-ingredient method

The quick-mix method is hands-down the easiest mixing method, requiring no special tools or equipment. It's used in scratch recipes, like the ones below, but it's also the method used when putting together a batch of box mix. In quick-mix recipes, the fats and other wet ingredients are combined in one bowl, while the dry are combined in another. The wet-into-dry or dry-into-wet debate will probably rage on among hardcore bakers for years to come, but my preference is to add the wet ingredients to the dry. Mix the batter in the center of the bowl and pull the dry ingredients into the wet. Either way, work the batter as little as possible to prevent too much gluten from developing, leaving you with a cake that has a dry, dense crumb.

» **Any Veggie Cake**

» **Any Fruit Cake**

» **Any Booze Cake**

Yields:
» *Just under 10 cups batter*
» *Two tall 8-inch round cakes*
» *Three regular 6-inch round cakes*

4½ cups all-purpose flour (plus more for the pans)

1½ teaspoons baking powder

¾ teaspoon baking soda

1 teaspoon kosher salt

6 large eggs

3 cups granulated sugar

1½ cups vegetable oil

¾ cup sour cream

1 teaspoon pure vanilla extract

Flavoring (see chart)

Shredded vegetable (see chart)

Fruit (see chart)

Nuts (see chart), optional

Any Veggie Cake

This recipe was born as a carrot cake, but evolved as I searched for a good zucchini cake recipe. Botanical purists, I see you wagging your fingers at me. Yes, zucchini is technically a fruit, but Any Root Veggie, Tuber, or Fleshy Thick-Skinned Fruit Cake just didn't have the same ring to it, you know? Basically, if you can grate it, it'll work with this recipe.

My perfect carrot cake includes pineapple, so my other veggie variations contain a complementary fruit as well. Pineapple perks up the veggie flavor and adds a much-needed hint of tartness. In all of these variations, the fruit can be omitted and replaced with an equal amount of additional shredded vegetables, though I strongly suggest enjoying the combinations as they are presented. The nuts are entirely optional. Include them for added texture, or omit if you're being mindful of allergies or creating a layered cake filled with an element of crunch.

///

1. Position a rack in the center of the oven and preheat to 350°F. Spray and flour pans in your chosen size.

2. In a large bowl, whisk together the flour, baking powder, baking soda, and salt.

3. In a separate medium bowl, whisk together the eggs, sugar, vegetable oil, sour cream, vanilla extract, and flavoring.

4. Pour the wet mixture into the dry ingredients and whisk until combined. Switch to a rubber spatula and fold in the shredded vegetable, fruit, and optional nuts.

UNICORN thought

Swap in extra-virgin olive oil for the vegetable oil. Olive oil is not only heart-healthy, it provides complexity to the cake with an added savory flavor and subtle floral notes.

5. Divide the batter evenly between the prepared pans and bake, rotating the pans' positions halfway through baking, until a toothpick inserted in the center of a cake comes out clean or with a few crumbs clinging to it, 50 to 55 minutes for 8-inch round pans or 35 to 40 minutes for 6-inch round pans.

6. Transfer the cakes to a rack to cool in the pan for about 30 minutes. Turn the cakes out onto a flat surface, like plates or a clean countertop. Let the cakes cool completely before frosting, filling, or storing.

SEE IT IN A SLICE: *page 148*

VEGGIE CAKE VARIATIONS

	FLAVORING	VEGETABLE	FRUIT	NUTS
Carrot Cake	1½ teaspoons ground cinnamon 1 teaspoon ground ginger ¼ teaspoon ground allspice ¼ teaspoon ground cloves	3 cups shredded carrots	1½ cups finely diced pineapple, fresh or canned (drained)	2 cups walnuts, toasted and chopped
Zucchini Cake	1 tablespoon grated lemon zest	3 cups drained shredded zucchini	1½ cups blueberries, fresh or frozen (unthawed)	2 cups almonds, toasted and chopped
Sweet Potato Cake	1 tablespoon ground cinnamon	3 cups shredded sweet potato	1½ cups finely diced peeled apple	2 cups pecans, toasted and chopped

I prefer to use a hand-grater that yields paper-thin vegetable strips. Pre-shredded carrots found in the produce section are too thick to properly disperse throughout the batter.

UNICORN thought

Any Fruit Cake

Yields:
» *10 cups batter*
» *Two tall 8-inch round cakes*
» *Three regular 6-inch round cakes*

4½ cups cake flour (plus more cake flour or all-purpose flour for the pans)

1 tablespoon baking powder

1½ teaspoons baking soda

1½ teaspoons cinnamon (see chart), optional

1½ teaspoons kosher salt

6 large eggs

3 cups granulated sugar

Fruit puree (see chart)

3 cups vegetable oil

1½ teaspoons pure vanilla extract

Cake is my favorite way to capture the flavor of a season. In New Hampshire, we have the good fortune of enjoying distinct seasons that each bring their own treasured bounty. It's all pretty magical, except for February and March. Then it's snowy and gray and there's not much going on in the way of fresh produce. That's when I turn to the freezer, either my own or the one at the supermarket. I'd like to say that I spend each season squirreling away pureed fresh fruits and vegetables, but let's be real—that doesn't always happen. Frozen fruits and vegetables have gotten a bad rap, but I'm not exactly sure why. They're flash frozen at the peak of ripeness, readily available at every supermarket and box store, and relatively inexpensive. Seems pretty great to me. Just be sure to buy frozen fruit or purees that have no added sugar. You can even check with local farms near you in the winter to see if they have any frozen fruits from the previous season's harvest.

1. Position a rack in the center of the oven and preheat to 350°F. Spray and flour pans in your chosen size.

2. In a large bowl, whisk together the cake flour, baking powder, baking soda, cinnamon (if using), and salt.

3. In a separate medium bowl, whisk together the eggs, sugar, fruit puree, vegetable oil, and vanilla extract.

FRUIT CAKE VARIATIONS

	FRUIT PUREE	CINNAMON (*optional*)
Strawberry Cake	2¼ cups strawberry puree	
Cherry Cake	2¼ cups cherry puree	
Banana Cake	2¼ cups mashed bananas	1½ teaspoons
Pumpkin Cake	2¼ cups pumpkin puree	1½ teaspoons
Applesauce Cake	2¼ cups unsweetened applesauce	1½ teaspoons

4. Pour the wet mixture into the dry ingredients and whisk until combined. When the batter becomes too thick to whisk, switch to a rubber spatula. Stir until the flour is completely incorporated.

5. Divide the batter evenly between the prepared pans and bake, rotating the pans' positions halfway through baking, until a toothpick inserted in the center of a cake comes out clean or with a few crumbs clinging to it, 40 to 45 minutes for 8-inch round pans or 25 to 30 minutes for 6-inch round pans.

6. Transfer the cakes to a rack to cool in the pan for about 30 minutes. Turn the cakes out onto a flat surface, like plates or a clean countertop. Let the cakes cool completely before frosting, filling, or storing.

SEE IT IN A SLICE: *page 179*

Save time and use store-bought puree, or make your own: Blend fresh fruit with a small amount of sugar (if needed) and cook the mixture over medium-high heat for 5 to 10 minutes to cook out the excess water. (Be sure to thaw frozen fruit overnight and discard the excess juices before blending and cooking down.)

UNICORN thought

12 ounces unsalted butter, softened

2 cups booze (see chart), plus more for your glass

2 cups packed dark brown sugar

2 cups granulated sugar

2 cups Dutch-processed cocoa powder

4 large eggs

1 cup sour cream

4 teaspoons pure vanilla extract

4 cups all-purpose flour (plus more for the pans)

1 tablespoon baking soda

2 teaspoons baking powder

2 teaspoons kosher salt

Red food coloring (see chart), optional

Any Booze Cake

At my bakery, the Chocolate Stout Cake was a favorite for groom's cakes. The rich beer flavor is there, but subtle. It acts as a supporting cast member to bring out the nutty flavor of the cocoa powder. Pair this cake with anything you'd typically drink with chocolate cake, or get the party started by finishing the cake with Baileys Buttercream (page 61), replicating the flavors of an Irish Car Bomb.

Another perennial favorite with couples was our Red Velvet Cake (page 38). However, I've never been the biggest fan of red velvet cake because most recipes are essentially a light cocoa cake with red food coloring. I am, however, a big fan of red wine. Brainstorming ways to incorporate wine into a cake recipe led me back to the chocolate stout cake. A his-and-hers of booze-y cakes, if you will. Cocoa powder + booze > cocoa powder + food coloring. In the red wine version, the wine flavor is definitely there. It is a decidedly adult cake. As is, the cake has a lovely, cocoa-ruby tinge to it. Add the food coloring if you must, but it's entirely unnecessary.

//

1. Position a rack in the center of the oven and preheat to 350°F. Spray and flour pans in your chosen size.

2. In a medium heatproof bowl, combine the butter and booze and heat in the microwave in 1 minute intervals to melt the butter. Or, combine the butter and booze in a medium saucepan over low heat to melt the butter. Add the dark brown and granulated sugars. Whisk to combine.

BOOZE CAKE VARIATIONS – – – – – – – – – – – – – – – – – –

	BOOZE	**RED FOOD COLORING** *(optional)*
Chocolate Stout Cake	2 cups stout	
Red Wine Cake	2 cups dry red wine	1 teaspoon

3. Add the cocoa powder to the butter mixture and whisk until combined. Add the eggs, sour cream, and vanilla extract and whisk until combined. If making the red wine cake, mix in the food coloring (if using).

4. In a separate large bowl, whisk together the flour, baking soda, baking powder, and salt.

5. Pour the wet mixture into the dry ingredients and whisk until combined. When the batter becomes too thick to whisk, switch to a rubber spatula. Stir until the flour is completely incorporated.

6. Divide the batter evenly between the prepared pans and bake, rotating the pans' positions halfway through baking, until a toothpick inserted in the center of a cake comes out clean or with a few crumbs clinging to it, 45 to 50 minutes for 8-inch round pans or 30 to 35 minutes for 6-inch round pans.

7. Transfer the cakes to a rack to cool in the pan for about 30 minutes. Turn the cakes out onto a flat surface, like plates or a clean countertop. Let the cakes cool completely before frosting, filling, or storing.

SEE IT IN A SLICE: *page 203*

Both versions of this recipe rely on the flavor of the alcohol you use. Buy the good stuff, but more specifically, buy the stuff you like to drink. No judgments on your brand preferences.

UNICORN thought

perfect pairings

What's your Cakequation? Follow my lead below, or create your own cakey, creamy, crunchy adventure.

CAKE	CREAMY	CRUNCHY
Blueberry Lemon Birthday Cake	Raspberry Buttercream	Almond Meringue
Espresso Birthday Cake	Chocolate Buttercream	Pistachio Brittle
Orange Clove Birthday Cake	Vanilla Buttercream, Rose Water Marshmallow	Raspberry Meringue
Toffee Birthday Cake	Salted Caramel Buttercream	Toffee
Funfetti Birthday Cake	Cream Cheese Frosting	White Chocolate–Coated Froot Loop Cereal Clusters
Chocolate Birthday Cake	Peanut Butter Buttercream	Candy-Coated Ritz Cracker Clusters
Black Velvet Birthday Cake	Peppermint Buttercream	Dark Chocolate–Coated Oreo Cookie Clusters
Almond Butter Cake	Vanilla Buttercream, Raspberry Jam	Lemon Meringue
Nutella Cake	Chocolate Buttercream	Hazelnut Butter Crunch
Sun Butter Cake	Chocolate Buttercream	Candied Sunflower Seed Crunch
Honey Pound Cake	Strawberry Buttercream	Pistachio Toffee
Gingerbread Pound Cake	Maple Buttercream	White Chocolate–Coated Gingersnap Cookie Clusters
Maple Pound Cake	Vanilla Buttercream	Chocolate Chips
Carrot Cake	Honey Buttercream	Macadamia Nut–Ginger Brittle
Zucchini Cake	Lemon Cream Cheese Frosting	Almond Toffee
Sweet Potato Cake	Brown Sugar Buttercream, Marshmallow	Candied Pecan Crunch
Strawberry Cake	Vanilla Buttercream, Dark Chocolate Ganache	Almond Toffee
Banana Cake	Chocolate Buttercream, Toasted Peanut Ganache	Peanut Toffee
Pumpkin Cake	Cinnamon Buttercream	Pumpkin Seed Brittle
Applesauce Cake	Maple Buttercream	Candied Walnut Crunch
Chocolate Stout Cake	Salted Caramel Buttercream	Whiskey Honeycomb Candy
Red Wine Cake	Blackberry Cabernet Buttercream	Chocolate Chips

CAKE   +   **CREAMY**   +   **CRUNCHY**

=

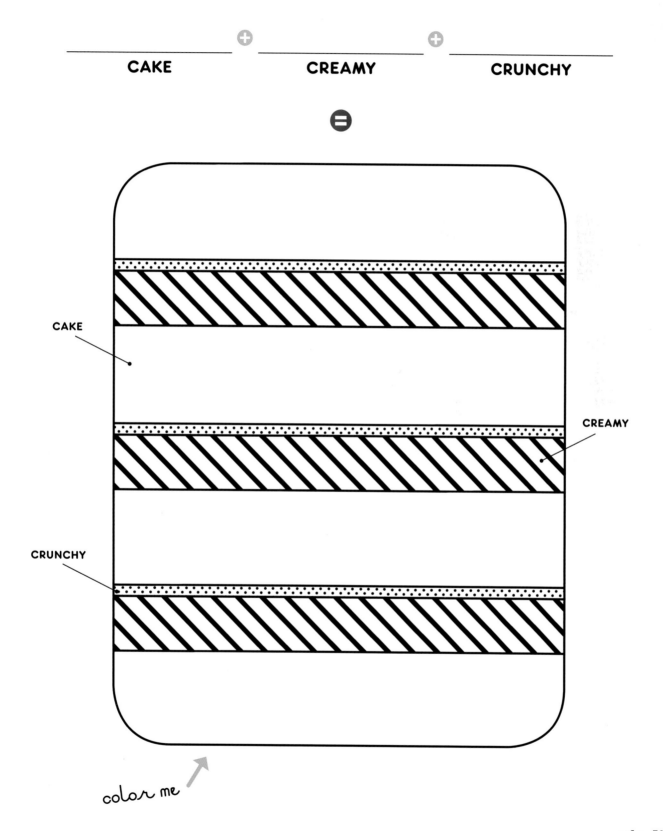

CAKE

CREAMY

CRUNCHY

color me

Chapter 4

....

CREAMY

END PIECES ARE MY FAVORITE. I'VE BEEN KNOWN TO TEAR off and toss away the bottom of a cupcake, and I always twist open sandwich cookies to get to the creamy filling. Cake is a wonderful thing, but in my world, its number-one reason for existence is to serve as a vehicle for delivering creamy deliciousness to my mouth.

In this section, I offer not only recipes for cake's best friend, buttercream, but other luscious fillings and potential finishes like ganache, cream cheese frosting, and even marshmallow. Supporting cast members like jam, caramel, and curd also pack a flavorful punch—just a thin layer can elevate a cake from simple to spectacular. For a decadent finishing touch, keep any extras nearby to individually sauce the slices as you serve them.

ALL THE BUTTERCREAM

In my experiences as a cake designer and instructor, I've learned that frosting preferences are very personal. I began life as a canned-frosting lover, became a Swiss meringue snob, and have now circled back to a place where I can appreciate the appeal of both and everything in between. Sometimes I'm feeling fancy and want a frosting that's light on the tongue and delicate in flavor. Sometimes I want something that's easy to make and satisfies my sweet tooth. Luckily, no matter what you're craving, there's a buttercream for that. In every Cakequation, when I say "buttercream," use the version that you enjoy most.

I added ermine frosting to my toolbox late in the game, and it was something of a revelation. Whipping softened butter with creamy pudding? Yes, please! I'll have some more. I adore Swiss meringue buttercream (aka SMBC), because of its airy texture and more sophisticated flavor, but standing over a double boiler isn't always my idea of a good time. In my recipe, I cook the sugar in the custard-making process, giving my ermine buttercream a texture similar in feel to SMBC, but without the double-boiler facial.

If you have dietary restrictions, substitutions for the fats or dairy can be made in all of these recipes. Instead of butter, use shortening or a butter-flavored vegan spread. Soy or almond milk can be swapped in for the whole milk—just be sure to pick up the plain kind with no added flavoring or sugar.

MEET THE BUTTERCREAMS

Each of my three favorite buttercream recipes have their own little personality quirks. Get to know them better before deciding which one to make for your cake project.

	PROS	CONS
Swiss Meringue Buttercream *AKA: SMBC*	Smooth as silk. Works beautifully as a cake finish and for piping details like flowers or pearls. SMBC is a very stable frosting and is the frosting of choice when filling and finishing fine wedding cakes. Works like a dream under fondant.	Requires time, patience, and practice to make. Using a double boiler and candy thermometer can be a bit of a pain. SMBC will soften quickly in warmer weather.
American Buttercream *AKA: AMBC or Crusting Buttercream*	Easy, quick, and a hit with kids. It also works well as a cake finish and for piping decorations. AMBC holds up well in warmer weather when made with at least 50 percent shortening.	Very sweet. AMBC can have more of a textured mouthfeel when compared to meringue frostings. When made with shortening, it can leave a greasy feel on the lips.
Ermine Buttercream *AKA: Flour Frosting or Cooked Milk Buttercream*	Easier to make than SMBC, but more steps than AMBC. It's a great compromise if AMBC is too sweet and gritty for you, but a meringue buttercream seems like too much trouble to make. It holds up well in warm weather, is easily piped, and works well under fondant.	It requires more steps than AMBC and more time for the custard to cool. While ermine frosting is smooth, it can have a thicker mouthfeel than a lighter meringue buttercream.

SEE IT IN
A SLICE:
page 165

Swiss Meringue Buttercream

AKA: SMBC

//

» *Yields 5 cups frosting*

½ cup pasteurized egg whites or 4 large egg whites

1 cup granulated sugar

¼ teaspoon kosher salt

16 ounces unsalted butter, cold and cut into small cubes

1 tablespoon pure vanilla extract

1. In a medium heatproof bowl, whisk together the egg whites, sugar, and salt. Heat the mixture in the microwave on high for 1 minute at a time, whisking after each interval, until the sugar has dissolved, 2 to 3 minutes. Or, heat the mixture over a double boiler, whisking occasionally, until the sugar has dissolved. If you're using fresh egg whites, heat the mixture until it measures 160°F on a candy thermometer.

2. Pour the egg mixture into the bowl of a stand mixer fitted with the whisk attachment (or a large bowl if using a hand mixer). Beat the egg whites on low speed just until the mixture starts to loosen and foam. Turn the mixer up to high speed and beat the egg whites until the mixture resembles a white, fluffy cloud, 8 to 10 minutes.

3. Turn the mixer down to low speed and add the butter, a few cubes at a time. The mixture will appear curdled, but that's OK. Once all the butter has been added, turn the mixer up to medium-high speed and beat until the buttercream is smooth, glossy, and light in color, 10 to 15 minutes.

4. Add the vanilla extract or other flavoring and mix until incorporated.

5. Use the buttercream immediately or store it in the fridge in an airtight container for up to a week. Press plastic wrap directly against the surface of the buttercream before putting the lid on the container to prevent it from absorbing fridge odors.

6. To bring cold buttercream back to a usable consistency, transfer it to a mixer fitted with the whisk attachment. Beat on medium-high speed until the buttercream is fluffy and spreadable again, about 15 minutes. The buttercream will break down and appear curdled again before it comes back together.

American Buttercream

AKA: AMBC OR CRUSTING BUTTERCREAM

SEE IT IN A SLICE: *page 203*

» *Yields 5 cups frosting*

16 ounces fat (butter, shortening, or 50/50 butter and shortening), softened

7½ cups (one 2-pound bag) confectioners' sugar

1 tablespoon pure vanilla extract

Pinch salt

2 to 4 tablespoons whole milk

1. In the bowl of a stand mixer fitted with the paddle attachment (or in a large bowl using an electric hand mixer), beat your chosen combination of softened fats on medium speed until light and fluffy. If you're using a combination of butter and shortening, beat the butter first until smooth, 5 minutes; add the shortening and beat until combined, about 5 minutes more.

2. With the mixer on low speed, slowly add the confectioners' sugar until just combined, stopping occasionally to scrape down the sides of the bowl with a rubber spatula, 5 to 7 minutes.

3. Turn off the mixer and add the vanilla extract and salt. Mix on low speed just until combined.

4. Keep the mixer on low speed and slowly add the milk, a tablespoon at a time, until the frosting reaches your desired consistency.

5. Use the buttercream immediately or store it in the fridge in an airtight container for up to a week. Press plastic wrap directly against the surface of the buttercream before putting the lid on the container to prevent it from forming a crust and absorbing fridge odors.

6. To bring cold buttercream back to a usable consistency, transfer it to a mixer fitted with the paddle attachment. Beat on medium-high speed until the buttercream is fluffy and spreadable again, 5 to 10 minutes.

Supermarket shortening does the job just fine, but for superior flavor and texture, give high-ratio shortening, like Sweetex, a try. It can be purchased online or in specialty cake decorating stores.

UNICORN thought

SEE IT IN A SLICE: *page 176*

» *Yields 5 cups frosting*

2½ cups whole milk

2½ cups granulated sugar

6 tablespoons cornstarch

¼ teaspoon kosher salt

1 tablespoon pure vanilla extract

20 ounces unsalted butter, softened

Ermine Buttercream

AKA: FLOUR FROSTING OR COOKED MILK BUTTERCREAM

➕ **DOCTOR, DOCTOR!** *Can't stand the heat? Don't make the custard! Use 2½ cups store-bought pudding or custard and pick up the recipe at step 4. Get creative and make up your own variations by using flavored pudding.*

1. In a medium heatproof bowl, whisk together the milk, sugar, cornstarch, and salt. Heat the mixture in the microwave on high for 2 minutes. Stir the mixture well with a rubber spatula. Repeat this process 2 or 3 times, until the mixture has thickened to the consistency of mayonnaise. The custard should hold a solid line while you run your finger across the spatula. Or, combine the ingredients in a medium saucepan and cook over medium-high heat, stirring constantly with a rubber spatula, until thickened, about 10 minutes.

2. Whisk the vanilla extract into the custard until just combined.

3. Pour the custard into a shallow bowl. Press plastic wrap against the surface of the custard and pop it in the fridge until it's cool to the touch, about 20 minutes. Remove the butter from the fridge (if you haven't done so already) and allow it to come to room temperature while the custard is cooling.

4. In the bowl of a stand mixer fitted with the paddle attachment (or in a large bowl using an electric hand mixer), beat the butter on medium-high speed until light and fluffy, about 5 minutes. Scrape down the sides of the bowl with a rubber spatula.

5. Turn the mixer to low speed and add the custard to the creamed butter, a little at a time, until fully incorporated. Turn the mixer up to medium-high and beat until light and fluffy, 3 to 5 minutes.

6. Use the buttercream immediately or store it in the fridge in an airtight container for up to a week. Press plastic wrap directly against the surface of the buttercream before putting the lid on the container to prevent it from absorbing fridge odors.

7. To bring cold buttercream back to a usable consistency, transfer it to a mixer fitted with the paddle attachment. Beat on medium-high speed until the buttercream is fluffy and spreadable again, 5 to 10 minutes.

Fun fact: *Cream cheese frosting likes to take all the credit, but ermine frosting is the original topping for red velvet cake.*

UNICORN thought

BUTTERCREAM VARIATIONS -

These variations work with all three buttercream recipes. Keep the sweetness level of the buttercream in mind when choosing a variation. Adding an ingredient to SMBC or ermine will taste similar but less sweet than adding the same ingredient to AMBC. Add the additional ingredients once the frosting has come together, unless otherwise noted.

SWEET

Chocolate Buttercream	Fold in 1 cup melted and slightly cooled dark chocolate (60% cacao or higher) until combined.
Salted Caramel Buttercream	Whip in ¾ cup caramel and 1 tablespoon flake sea salt.
Brown Sugar Buttercream	SMBC and Ermine: Replace half of the granulated sugar with packed dark brown sugar. AMBC: Replace 2 cups of the confectioners' sugar with packed dark brown sugar.
Honey Buttercream	SMBC and Ermine: Replace half of the granulated sugar with honey. AMBC: Replace 1 cup of the confectioners' sugar with honey.
Maple Buttercream	SMBC and Ermine: Replace half of the granulated sugar with pure maple syrup. AMBC: Replace 1 cup of the confectioners' sugar with pure maple syrup.

NUTTY

Peanut Butter Buttercream	SMBC and Ermine: Whip in 1 cup smooth peanut butter. Increase the salt to ½ teaspoon. AMBC: Replace half of the fat with an equal amount of peanut butter. Reduce the confectioners' sugar to 4 cups. Increase the salt to ½ teaspoon.
Nutella Buttercream	Whip in ¾ cup chilled Nutella.
Halva Buttercream	SMBC and Ermine: Replace half of the granulated sugar with honey. Whip in ½ cup tahini paste. AMBC: Replace 1 cup of the confectioners' sugar with honey. Whip in ½ cup tahini paste.
Pistachio Buttercream	Whip in 1 cup pistachio paste. Increase the salt to ½ teaspoon.
Sunflower Seed Butter Buttercream	Whip in 1 cup sunflower seed butter. Increase the salt to ½ teaspoon.

FRUITY

Lemon or Lime Buttercream	Whip in 1 cup Lemon or Lime Curd (page 65). If you like, add the grated zest of either fruit for added texture and flavor.
Lemon Sherry Buttercream	Whip in 1 cup Lemon Curd (page 65) and ¼ cup cream sherry.
Any Berry Buttercream	Whip in 1 cup fruit preserves or jam (page 68).
Blackberry Cabernet Buttercream	Whip in 1 cup blackberry preserves and ¼ cup cabernet wine.
Coconut Buttercream	Whip in ¾ cup cream of coconut.

SEASONED

Cinnamon Buttercream	Whip in 1 tablespoon ground cinnamon.
Peppermint Buttercream	Whip in 1 teaspoon peppermint extract and ½ cup finely crushed peppermint candies.
Ginger Buttercream	Whip in ¾ cup ginger preserves. Strain out chunks of candied ginger for a smooth frosting.
Espresso Buttercream	Whip in 2 tablespoons Medaglia d'Oro instant espresso powder.
Baileys, Kahlúa, or Frangelico Buttercream	Whip in ½ cup liqueur.

» *Yields 2 cups ganache*

3 cups chopped dark chocolate (60% or higher, 72% preferred)

2 tablespoons Lyle's Golden Syrup (or light corn syrup)

Pinch kosher salt

2 cups heavy cream

Ganache

The very first restaurant I worked in had the most beautiful little chocolate bombes on the dessert menu. Being totally green, I had absolutely no idea how they were made and was desperate to find out. I convinced the pastry chef to let me tag along as he glazed a sheet of frozen bombes. On pins and needles, I waited for the big reveal. There had to be magic involved.

He boiled some cream, poured it over chocolate, gave it a quick whisk, and said to me, "You think you can do that?" Um, yeah. The experience wasn't quite as magical as I had hoped, but it was a revelation. There was no mystery ingredient or pastry-Jedi sleight of hand. It was just the right technique applied to a few quality ingredients.

Ganache is so simple, but still so elegant. Once you start, you'll end up making it all the time. Once you try one of the infusions, there's no turning back. You'll be tossing things into cream left and right just to see what happens. Buttered popcorn ganache? Yep, it works.

Silky smooth ganache relies on a delicate balance of fats and solids to create an emulsion. Dark, milk, and white chocolates all have different ratios of each, so the amount of cream needs to be adjusted based on which one you're using (see the variations below).

Besides being a luscious filling, ganache also acts as a versatile cake finish. Whip it, drip it, or slather it on. See page 100 for instructions on finishing a cake with ganache.

GANACHE VARIATIONS

Milk Chocolate Ganache	Use 1½ cups heavy cream.
White Chocolate Ganache	Use 1 cup heavy cream.
Coating Chocolate	Use 1 cup heavy cream.

**SEE IT IN
A SLICE:**
page 165

1. In a medium heatproof bowl, combine the chocolate, syrup, and salt.

2. In a small saucepan, bring the cream to a boil over medium-high heat.

3. Remove from the heat and pour the hot cream over the chocolate mixture. Whisk until the ingredients are completely combined and the chocolate has melted. If the mixture cools before the chocolate has completely melted, set the bowl over a saucepan of simmering water and gently warm while whisking until smooth.

4. Use fresh ganache as a sauce or to glaze a chilled, buttercream-coated cake. Let the ganache cool for about 30 minutes before using as a filling. To use as a cake filling, spread a thin layer of ganache onto a layer of cake. To fill with a thicker layer of ganache, first pipe a dam of buttercream around the edges of the cake layer to prevent the ganache from seeping out.

5. Store ganache in the fridge in an airtight container for up to a week. Press plastic wrap directly against the surface of the ganache before putting the lid on the container to prevent it from forming a skin and absorbing fridge odors.

6. Reheat ganache in the microwave in short intervals, 15 to 20 seconds, stirring in between.

★ *Lyle's Golden Syrup is the UK's greatest gift to the world (IMHO). It's a sweet, caramel-y, pure sugar cane syrup that will leave you saying, "Corn syrup, who?" Find it in the baking section of finer supermarkets and online.*

★ *If your ganache goes out of whack and breaks (the fats and solids separate), whisk in cold cream, a tablespoon at a time, until the ganache smoothes back out.*

UNICORN thought

GANACHE INFUSIONS - - - - - - - - - - - - - - - - - -

Infusing ganache is a fun way to add even more flavor to a cake filling or finish. Sounds fancy, but it couldn't be easier. At the end of step 2, steep the additional ingredients in the warm cream, covered, for 20 minutes. Strain before pouring over the chopped chocolate.

	DARK CHOCOLATE GANACHE	MILK CHOCOLATE GANACHE	WHITE CHOCOLATE GANACHE
SWEET			
Buttered Popcorn Ganache	1 cup popcorn and 2 tablespoons salted butter	¾ cup popcorn and 1 tablespoon salted butter	½ cup popcorn and 1½ teaspoons salted butter
Licorice Ganache	1 cup chopped black licorice	¾ cup chopped black licorice	½ cup chopped black licorice
NUTTY			
Toasted Peanut Ganache	1 cup toasted peanuts	¾ cup toasted peanuts	½ cup toasted peanuts
Hazelnut Ganache	1 cup hazelnut paste	¾ cup hazelnut paste	½ cup hazelnut paste
FRUITY			
Berry Ganache	1 cup crushed berries (assorted or a single kind)	¾ cup crushed berries (assorted or a single kind)	½ cup crushed berries (assorted or a single kind)
Citrus Ganache	Grated zest of 2 citrus fruits (assorted or a single kind)	Grated zest of 1 citrus fruit	Grated zest of ½ citrus fruit
SEASONED			
Tea Ganache	2 bags Earl Grey or chai tea	1 bag Earl Grey or chai tea	1 bag Earl Grey or chai tea
Espresso Ganache	2 tablespoons instant espresso powder	1 tablespoon instant espresso powder	1 teaspoon instant espresso powder

- -

Citrus Curd

I very clearly remember the day I learned that lemon curd could be made in the microwave. It was that big of a deal at the bakery. As a group, we loved things that were simple, delicious, and easy to throw together in 15 minutes. You could make this the old-fashioned way, standing with a whisk over a double boiler, but I encourage you to try it my way. Come to the dark side—we have lemon curd.

➕ **DOCTOR, DOCTOR!** *Customize store-bought curd by stirring in a tablespoon of jam.*

1. In a large microwave-safe bowl, whisk together the citrus juice, egg, egg yolks, sugar, butter, and salt.

2. Microwave the mixture on high for 1 minute. Whisk the mixture to distribute the heat. Repeat the heating and whisking process 4 or 5 times, until the mixture has thickened to the consistency of Greek yogurt. The curd may appear runnier than when cooked in a double boiler, but it will set up firm once chilled. Whisk in the vanilla extract.

3. Warm curd can be used as a sauce right away, or pour it into an airtight container and store in the fridge for up to a week. Press plastic wrap directly against the surface of the curd before putting the lid on the container to prevent it from forming a skin and absorbing fridge odors.

4. Allow the curd to cool completely before using as cake filling or to flavor buttercream. If using as cake filling, first pipe a buttercream dam around the edges of the cake layer to prevent the curd from oozing out.

SEE IT IN A SLICE: *page 123*

» *Yields 1½ cups curd*

Citrus juice (see chart)

1 large egg

3 large egg yolks

⅔ cup granulated sugar

2 ounces butter, cubed

Pinch salt

½ teaspoon pure vanilla extract

CITRUS CURD VARIATIONS

Lemon Curd	¾ cup lemon juice
Lime Curd	¾ cup lime juice
Orange Curd	½ cup orange juice and ¼ cup lemon juice
Grapefruit Curd	½ cup grapefruit juice and ¼ cup lemon juice

SEE IT IN
A SLICE:
page 148

Cream Cheese Frosting

I have a relationship with cream cheese frosting. I just wanted to put that out there from the start so you know where we stand. Its tangy-sweetness is the perfect complement to such a wide variety of cakes: strawberry, pumpkin, carrot, espresso, chocolate, red wine, banana, cherry, chocolate stout . . . to name more than a few. Can you tell I like cream cheese frosting?

Many recipes call for beating the butter and cream cheese at the same time, but doing that makes the frosting too soft. Butter and cream cheese are different animals. Beating air into butter makes it light and fluffy. Beating cream cheese to death causes it to separate and become runny or broken. Beating the butter before adding the cream cheese makes for a more stable frosting that works as both a filling and a frosting. It's sturdy enough for a simple finish, but not quite strong enough to hold up to elaborate piping.

» *Yields 5 cups
frosting*

16 ounces unsalted butter

16 ounces cream cheese, room temperature

1 bag (2 pounds) confectioners' sugar

1 tablespoon pure vanilla extract

1. In the bowl of a stand mixer fitted with the paddle attachment (or in a large bowl if using an electric hand mixer), beat the butter on medium-high speed until it's light and fluffy, about 5 minutes. Stop to scrape down the sides of the bowl with a rubber spatula.

2. On medium speed, add the cream cheese until just combined, about 3 minutes more.

3. Turn the mixer to low speed and add the confectioners' sugar, about 1 cup at a time, and mix until incorporated.

4. Add the vanilla extract and mix until combined.

5. Use the frosting immediately or store it in the fridge in an airtight container for up to a week. Press plastic wrap directly against the surface of the frosting before putting the lid on the container to prevent it from forming a crust and absorbing fridge odors.

6. To bring cold cream cheese frosting back to a usable consistency, transfer it to a mixer fitted with the paddle attachment (or large bowl if using an electric hand mixer). Beat on medium speed for just a minute or two, until the frosting is fluffy and spreadable again. Be careful not to overwhip.

7. If using as a cake filling, you may want to first pipe a dam of buttercream around the edges of the cake layer to prevent the cream cheese frosting from bulging out.

CREAM CHEESE FROSTING VARIATIONS – – – – – – – – – – – – – –

Brown Butter Cream Cheese Frosting	Brown the butter in a saucepan over medium-high heat. Pour the melted butter into a heatproof container, scraping in all the little browned bits with a rubber spatula. Allow the butter to completely re-harden in the refrigerator before proceeding with the recipe.
Citrus Cream Cheese Frosting	Whip in 4 teaspoons citrus juice and 1 tablespoon grated citrus zest (assorted or a single kind).
Berry Cream Cheese Frosting	Whip in ½ cup preserves (assorted or a single kind).

» *Yields about*
2 cups jam

3 cups chopped fruit (see chart on page 70)

½ cup granulated sugar (approximately)

Pinch salt

1 apple slice, peeled (optional)

Liquid (see chart on page 70), optional

Seasoning (see chart on page 70), optional

1 large lemon wedge

Jam

I got into jamming when I worked as pastry chef at a big old inn here in New Hampshire. The owner of the big old inn liked to throw me challenges. Shortly after my arrival, he informed me that he had always dreamed of the jam for breakfast being made on site. Oh, and not just one jam, *three* jams served to every guest as they sit down at the breakfast table. A spread of jams. And they should change daily. Oh! And reflect the seasons here in NH. Except apple season—always have an apple jam. Oh, and I like pineapples, too. Yeah, that's it.

So, I learned how to jam. I jammed out. I was jammin'. Once I got the hang of it, I got cocky and started creating jam combinations that might not immediately come to mind when you think about downing a PB&J. Combos like pineapple-lime or spiced carrot. Strawberry red-wine jam might not be for the kiddies, but it sure is good on waffles at brunch. Not to mention whipped into a buttercream.

This is the faster and easier version of that jam. Fast jam, jam in a flash. It's sometimes called refrigerator jam or freezer jam. It's a great gateway jam, if you've always been curious about canning, but afraid to ask. No need for additional pectin; the lemon rind and apple slice provide enough natural pectin to keep the jam thick and gelled. Since we're not canning in the traditional sense (adding pectin, boiling jars, etc.), this jam will need to be stored in the refrigerator, where it will remain fresh for up to a week.

Jam is more of a technique and less of a recipe. The exact amount of sugar and the cook time will depend on how ripe and sweet your fruit is. Underripe fruit actually has more pectin in it than overripe fruit, which has more sugar. Jamming is a terrific use for fruit that never achieved its full potential sitting on your countertop. Jam on.

➕ **DOCTOR, DOCTOR!** *If you're too tired to jam, store-bought jams work for every recipe in this book that calls for jam. Farmers' markets and health food stores are great places to find jams made with local fruit in interesting flavor combinations.*

SEE IT IN A SLICE: *page 195*

1. Place something ceramic or metal in the freezer (plate, bowl, spoons, cookie sheet, etc.) for testing the jam later.

2. In a medium saucepan, combine the chopped fruit, sugar, salt, apple slice, optional liquid, and additional seasoning. Squeeze the juice from the lemon wedge into the pot and toss in the rind as well.

3. Bring the pan to a simmer over medium-high heat. Cook the jam for 15 to 30 minutes, until it's thick and forms gelatinous puddles when drizzled on a cold plate or cookie sheet. The jam should hold a line when you run your finger through it. Remove the lemon rind with a pair of tongs and discard.

4. Allow the jam to cool completely and store in an airtight container in the fridge for up to a week. Press plastic wrap directly against the surface of the jam before putting the lid on the container to prevent it from forming a skin and absorbing fridge odors.

5. If using as a cake filling, spread a thin layer of jam onto a layer of cake before topping with another creamy filling or another layer of cake.

JAM COMBINATIONS ------------------------------

Now that you know how to jam, it's time to freestyle. Choose your fruit from along the top and look for the star next to the liquid(s) or seasoning(s) that pair best with it. For example, red-wine berry jam? Rockstar. Pineapple balsamic jam? Not on my toast, thanks.

	BERRIES *(assorted or a single kind)*	CHERRIES, *pitted*	APRICOTS, *pitted*
OPTIONAL LIQUID			
Red wine, 1 cup	★	★	
White wine, 1 cup	★		★
Beer, 1 cup			
Apple cider, 1 cup	★	★	★
Rosé, 1 cup	★	★	★
Cranberry juice, 1 cup			
Champagne, 1 cup	★	★	★
Orange juice, 1 cup	★		★
Maple syrup, 1/2 cup	★	★	
OPTIONAL SEASONING			
Cinnamon, 1 stick or 1 tablespoon ground	★	★	
Ginger, 1 tablespoon grated fresh or ground	★	★	★
Any citrus, 2 tablespoons juice and 1 tablespoon zest	★	★	★
Liqueur (Baileys, Kahlúa, Frangelico, St-Germain) or rum, 1 tablespoon or to taste	★	★	★
Ground black pepper, 1 tablespoon or to taste	★	★	
Balsamic vinegar, 2 tablespoons	★	★	
Tea (chai, Earl Grey, herbal), 2 tablespoons	★	★	★
Fresh herbs (thyme, basil, lavender), 2 tablespoons	★	★	★

PINEAPPLE, peeled and cored	APPLES, peeled and cored	PEARS, peeled and cored	FIGS	GRAPES	PEACHES, pitted and peeled
			★	★	
★	★	★		★	★
	★		★		
	★	★	★	★	★
	★	★		★	★
	★	★			
★	★	★	★	★	★
★					
	★	★	★		
	★	★	★	★	
★	★	★	★	★	★
★	★	★	★	★	★
★	★	★	★	★	★
★			★	★	
	★	★	★	★	
	★	★		★	★
★	★	★	★	★	★

» *Yields 2 cups*
pastry cream

6 large egg yolks

⅔ cup granulated sugar

3 tablespoons cornstarch

Pinch kosher salt

2 cups whole milk

1 tablespoon unsalted butter

1 tablespoon pure vanilla extract

Pastry Cream
AKA: PARTY CREAM

When I owned my cake shop, I probably spent half of my time writing e-mails: answering inquiries about cakes, talking details about wedding cakes, setting up deliveries, etc. They never stopped. I'd answer one and two more would pop up. It was all pretty monotonous, until one day I received the greatest e-mail of all-time from a panicked mother-of-the-groom. She was freaking out over the flavor combinations for her son's wedding cake. (Not her wedding cake, but whatever.) Will the party cream go with the cake flavors they've chosen? Can we flavor the party cream? Will the party cream spoil if the cake is at room temperature? Can you show me a picture of the party cream? I had no idea what this woman was talking about for a good 10 minutes, until I realized her autocorrect had changed *pastry* to *party* throughout the entire email. I was stressed out and overtired, so it made me laugh like a hyena. It gave the other ladies in the shop a giggle as well. Pastry cream was known as party cream from there on out.

➕ **DOCTOR, DOCTOR!** *For a fluffy, mousse-like cake filling in a flash, combine one 3.5-ounce box of instant pudding mix (any kind) with 1 quart of heavy cream. Whip the powder and cream to stiff peaks. Chill until set.*

For a creamier, custard-like filling, make the instant pudding according to the box's directions, but with half as much milk. Add even more richness by replacing the milk with heavy cream.

PASTRY CREAM VARIATIONS - - - - - - - - - - - - - - - -

Chocolate Pastry Cream	Whisk ½ cup chopped dark chocolate into the hot pastry cream along with the butter and vanilla extract in step 4.
Berry Pastry Cream	Add ¼ to ½ cup fresh berries (assorted or a single kind) to the milk before cooking in step 2. Mash the berries with the end of the spatula as they soften in the warm milk.
Citrus Pastry Cream	Add 1 tablespoon grated citrus zest and 2 tablespoons citrus juice (an assortment or a single kind) to the milk before warming in step 2.

1. In a large heatproof bowl, whisk together the egg yolks, sugar, cornstarch, and salt.

2. Pour the milk into a small saucepan and bring to a boil over medium-high heat. Remove from the heat. Slowly add half of the milk to the egg mixture while whisking vigorously to combine. Pour the tempered egg mixture back into the hot milk.

3. Cook over medium-low heat, stirring constantly with a spatula, until thickened (about the texture of mayonnaise), about 5 minutes. The pastry cream should hold a line when you run your finger through it on the back of the spatula.

4. Strain the pastry cream through a fine-mesh strainer into a storage container. Whisk in the butter and vanilla extract.

5. Press plastic wrap directly against the surface of the pastry cream before putting the lid on the container to prevent it from forming a skin and absorbing fridge odors. Store the pastry cream in the fridge for 2 to 3 days.

6. If using as a cake filling, first pipe a dam of buttercream around the edges of the cake layer to prevent the pastry cream from smooshing out between layers.

★ *Save those extra egg whites to whip up some gorgeous meringue decorations (pages 175 and 177) or to add crunchy meringue bits to your cake layers (page 86).*

★ *Slow is the way to go when adding anything warm to eggs or egg yolks. Adding a small amount of hot milk to the egg yolks helps to temper the mixture so that your party cream doesn't become scrambled eggs.*

UNICORN thought

» *Yields 2 cups caramel*

3 cups granulated sugar

1 cup water

Pinch cream of tartar

1½ cups heavy cream

½ vanilla bean (split and seeded), or 1 teaspoon pure vanilla extract

½ teaspoon kosher salt

1½ teaspoons dark rum (optional)

1½ teaspoons orange juice (optional)

6 ounces unsalted butter

Caramel

I learned this caramel from the first pastry chef I ever worked for. He was an accidental pastry chef, brought to the restaurant we worked at through some sort of circumstance that was never entirely clear to me. He was smart and curious with a sharp sense of humor . . . and was an incredible pain in the ass. I know he didn't know it, but the kindness and generosity he showed me in the time I worked for him fueled me through my entire pastry career. His English was broken and his techniques were cobbled together from his own experimentation. I wish I could replicate my experience with him for every person looking to become a pastry chef, because I could not think of a better introduction to the restaurant world.

I don't know how he came to combine this series of ingredients for caramel, but it works. The orange juice and rum can be omitted, but please try it at least once. You won't be able to taste either ingredient on its own. The acidity from the juice and the sugar in the rum just help to boost the rich, caramel flavor.

➕ **DOCTOR, DOCTOR!** *Head to the ice cream aisle and pick up a jar of caramel sundae topping. Simply warm the store-bought caramel in the microwave. You can also customize it with any of the variations from the chart.*

1. In a large saucepan, combine the sugar, water, and cream of tartar. If you're using a vanilla bean, add it at this point. Cook over medium-high heat without stirring until dark amber in color, 10 to 15 minutes.

2. Remove the pan from the heat and wait until the caramel stops bubbling. Carefully whisk in the heavy cream. The caramel will sputter and release steam as the cold cream is added, so don't add the cream with your face directly above the pan.

3. Whisk in the salt, rum, orange juice, and butter until combined. If using vanilla extract, whisk it in now. If you used a vanilla bean, fish out the pod with a fork or pair of tongs and discard.

4. Allow the caramel to cool completely before using as a cake filling or to flavor buttercream. Warm caramel can be used right away as a sauce.

5. Pour the caramel into an airtight heatproof container and store it in the fridge for up to a week. Press plastic wrap directly against the surface of the caramel before putting the lid on the container to prevent it from forming a skin and absorbing fridge odors.

6. To use as a cake filling, spread a thin layer of caramel onto a layer of cake. To fill with a thicker layer of caramel, first pipe a dam of buttercream around the edges of the cake layer to prevent the caramel from seeping out.

SEE IT IN A SLICE: *page 131*

CARAMEL VARIATIONS

Chocolate Caramel	Whisk ½ cup chopped dark chocolate into the warm caramel after adding the butter in step 3.
Salted Caramel	Replace the salt with 2 tablespoons flaky sea salt.
Cabernet Caramel	Replace ¾ cup of the heavy cream with red wine.

» *Yields 1 layer of filling for an 8-inch round cake or about 3 cups*

Cooking spray

Cornstarch, for dusting the pan and marshmallow

½ cup cold water

1 teaspoon pure vanilla extract

5 teaspoons unflavored powdered gelatin

¾ cup water

2 teaspoons Lyle's Golden Syrup or corn syrup

2 cups granulated sugar

Marshmallow

"You can make that?"

That's the first thing anyone ever says to me when they see homemade marshmallow for the first time. So much so that it became a running joke between my sister and me at the bakery. It's one of those things that many people don't ever think about making on their own, but you should. Fresh marshmallow is head and shoulders above its barrel-shaped cousins at the supermarket. It's lighter and fluffier with superior flavor, thanks to pure vanilla extract and a lack of preservatives.

A candy thermometer would be useful here, but it's not entirely necessary. To test the sugar's doneness, carefully drizzle a few drops of the hot sugar onto a cold plate or into a glass of cold water. If you can roll a drop into a ball between your fingertips, you've reached soft ball. If the drips firm up solid, you've reached hard crack.

➕ **DOCTOR, DOCTOR!** *Fill the prepared pan with store-bought marshmallows nestled in tightly together. Warm the pan in a hot oven (350°F) for 8 to 10 minutes, until the marshmallows have melted together. Follow the same directions for dusting, cooling, and filling.*

1. Spray an 8-inch round pan with cooking spray and dust with cornstarch.

2. In the bowl of a stand mixer fitted with the whisk attachment (or in a large bowl if using an electric hand mixer), combine the cold water, vanilla extract, and powdered gelatin.

3. In a medium saucepan, combine the ¾ cup water, golden syrup, and sugar. Cook over medium-high heat until the mixture reaches soft ball stage or 235°F on a candy thermometer, about 10 minutes. If you don't have a thermometer, test the sugar for doneness once the bubbles start to slow and the mixture begins to thicken but is still clear. Drizzle a drop of the sugar into a glass of cold water or onto a cold plate. The ball should firm up but remain malleable. Remove the pan from the heat.

4. With the mixer on low speed, slowly and carefully pour the hot sugar over the bloomed gelatin. Once all of the sugar has been added, turn the mixer up to medium-high speed and whip until it's soft, fluffy, and glossy white, about 10 minutes.

5. Quickly pour the warm marshmallow into the prepared pan. Sprinkle the surface of the marshmallow with cornstarch and use your hand to smooth it down. Allow it to set completely before using, about 30 minutes (or pop the marshmallow in the fridge to speed up the process). You can also pour warm marshmallow into a piping bag and pipe shapes onto parchment paper or directly onto a cake.

6. Once firm, turn the marshmallow out of the pan and layer between cakes to use as a filling. Spread a thin layer of buttercream or ganache on the cake layers above and below the marshmallow layer to help it stick.

SEE IT IN A SLICE: *page 157*

MARSHMALLOW VARIATIONS - - - - - - - - - - - - - - - -

Peppermint Marshmallow	Add ½ teaspoon peppermint extract to the gelatin, vanilla, and water mixture in step 2. Add ½ cup crushed peppermint candies to the whipping marshmallow in step 4, after the hot sugar has been added.
Chocolate Marshmallow	Pour ½ cup melted dark chocolate into the whipping marshmallow in step 4, after the hot sugar has been added.
Berry Marshmallow	Add ¼ cup jam or preserves (assorted or a single kind) to the whipping marshmallow in step 4, after the hot sugar has been added.
Caramel Swirl Marshmallow	Fold ½ cup cooled caramel (page 74) into the finished marshmallow at the end of step 4, before pouring into the prepared pan.
Rose Water Marshmallow	Add ¼ teaspoon rose water to the gelatin, vanilla, and water mixture in step 2.

Chapter 5

····································

CRUNCHY

I'VE ALWAYS FELT THE ROLE OF A PASTRY CHEF IS TO create something craveable. As the closer, it's my job to keep everyone coming back for more. You have to eat dinner—dessert should be something you dream about. When imagining a composed dessert, I combine flavors and textures in a way that is both pleasurable and interesting. Smooth, creamy components are almost always balanced by an element of crunch. Crème brûlée is arguably a perfect dessert. Why? That *crunch*. When I moved into the wedding cake world, my beloved crunch was nowhere to be found. What the crunch?

Yes, I know this puts another step between you and cake. Trust me, it's worth it! Adding an element of crunch can be as simple as tossing a handful of mini chocolate chips into your buttercream, or as fancy and fussy as topping your layers of filling with a sprinkling of homemade meringue batons.

Oh, and here's a little secret: The recipes in this chapter aren't just layer cake components, they're also *snacks*. Yes! I hid an entire chapter on snacks in my cake book. Tee hee! When making any of the layer Cakequations in Eye Candy (starting on page 93) or from Perfect Pairings (page 50), make the crunch element first. Then you'll have fuel to get you through the rest of your cakey-bakey tasks.

**SEE IT IN
A SLICE:**
page 207

» *Yields 2 cups
candied nuts
or seeds*

**2 cups nuts or
seeds (see chart
on page 83)**

**½ cup granulated
sugar**

**2 teaspoons
seasoning (see
chart on page 83)**

**½ teaspoon kosher
salt**

1 large egg white

Candied Crunch

Many of the recipes in this chapter, like this one, are more a process
than a strict recipe. Use the candied nuts to garnish a plated slice of
cake, or finely chop them and add to your cake layers. Use plain,
un-toasted nuts and seeds in this recipe since they will be baked
once coated.

1. Position a rack in the center of the oven and preheat to 350°F. Line
a cookie sheet with parchment paper or a silicone baking mat.

2. In a large bowl, combine the nuts, sugar, seasoning, and salt.

3. In a separate small bowl, whisk the egg white until foamy. Pour
the egg white over the nut mixture and toss to combine. Pour the nut
mixture onto the prepared cookie sheet.

4. Bake for 10 to 15 minutes, shaking the pan halfway through
baking so that the nuts don't stick, until golden amber in color.

5. Allow the nuts to cool completely and store them in an airtight
container in a cool, dry place for up to 2 weeks.

6. If using in a cake filling, finely chop the candied crunch and
sprinkle onto a cake layer that's been topped with buttercream or
another creamy filling. Top the creamy, crunchy filling with another
layer of cake.

UNICORN
thought

*To make honey-roasted crunchy bits, replace half of
the sugar with honey.*

Toffee

This just might be the easiest, most addictive thing I know how to make. Toffee can sometimes be sticky or tough to chew, but this recipe makes a candy that is glossy, smooth, and pleasantly crunchy. Toffee is denser, thinner, and more buttery than brittle. It makes a great addition to cake batter, leaving behind crunchy pockets of goodness. No need to break out the candy thermometer! The toffee is ready to pour once it's golden and bubbly. Finely chop the toffee before adding to your cake layers, folding into buttercream, or stirring into cake batter before baking.

➕ **DOCTOR, DOCTOR!** *Buy a bag of toffee pieces in the baking aisle at the supermarket. Create a custom blend by adding chopped toasted nuts or seeds.*

//

1. Line a cookie sheet with parchment paper or a silicone baking mat.

2. In a small saucepan, combine the butter, sugar, and salt. Cook over medium-high heat, whisking occasionally, until golden and bubbly, 5 to 7 minutes. Remove the pan from the heat and stir in the nuts or seeds and optional seasoning with a heatproof rubber spatula. Pour onto the prepared cookie sheet.

3. Allow the toffee to cool completely before breaking into chunks or chopping. Store in an airtight container in a cool, dry place for up to 2 weeks.

4. If using in a cake filling, finely chop the toffee and sprinkle onto a cake layer that's been topped with buttercream or another creamy filling. Top the creamy, crunchy filling with another layer of cake.

> *Toasting nuts helps to draw out their natural oils and release more flavor. Get your nuts toasty in a dry saucepan over medium heat or on an unlined cookie sheet in a hot (350° to 400°F) oven, shaking the pan frequently to prevent the nuts from burning, 5 to 8 minutes.*

SEE IT IN A SLICE: *page 113*

» *Yields 2 cups finely chopped toffee*

4 ounces unsalted butter

1 cup granulated sugar

1 teaspoon salt

1 cup chopped toasted nuts or seeds (see chart on page 83), optional

1 teaspoon seasoning (see chart on page 83), optional

UNICORN thought

» *Yields 2 cups finely chopped brittle*

½ cup granulated sugar

¼ cup water

3 tablespoons light corn syrup

1 teaspoon kosher salt

½ cups nuts or seeds (see chart)

1 tablespoon unsalted butter

1 teaspoon pure vanilla extract

1 teaspoon seasoning (see chart)

¾ teaspoon baking soda

Brittle

Brittle is similar to toffee in that it's a crispy cooked candy made with butter, but the addition of a single ingredient changes the candy entirely—baking soda. Baking soda reacts with the sugar acids and creates carbon dioxide, which causes the mixture to foam, puff up, and remain aerated when hardened. Use plain, un-toasted nuts and seeds in this recipe since they will be warmed in the sugar mixture. Finely chop brittle before adding it to your cake layers or using it to garnish a plated slice of cake.

1. Line a cookie sheet with greased parchment paper, foil, or a silicone baking mat.

2. In a medium saucepan, combine the sugar, water, corn syrup, and salt. Cook over medium-high heat until the mixture reaches hard ball consistency, or 265°F on a candy thermometer, 10 to 15 minutes. Stir in the nuts or seeds and cook until the mixture reaches hard crack consistency, 300°F on a candy thermometer, about 5 minutes more.

3. Remove the pan from the heat and immediately stir in the butter, vanilla extract, and seasoning until combined. Add the baking soda last (the mixture will bubble and foam when the baking soda is added, but fall slightly as you stir). Pour onto the prepared cookie sheet.

UNICORN thought

Use a slightly larger saucepan than what you think you'll need. You'll be thankful for the extra space after the baking soda is added and the mixture grows to 2 to 3 times its original size.

4. Allow the brittle to cool completely before breaking into chunks or chopping. Store in an airtight container in a cool, dry place for up to 2 weeks.

5. If using in a cake filling, finely chop the brittle and sprinkle onto a cake layer that's been topped with buttercream or another creamy filling. Top the creamy, crunchy filling with another layer of cake.

SEE IT IN A SLICE: *page 139*

CANDIED CRUNCH, TOFFEE, AND BRITTLE VARIATIONS – – – – – – –

Use plain, untoasted nuts or seeds for the Candied Crunch and Brittle recipes, because the nuts or seeds will be toasted at some point within the recipe. Toast your nuts or seeds when making Toffee, since they're folded in off heat. Mix and match the nuts, seeds, and seasonings to create your own crunchy, spicy adventure.

TOASTED NUTS OR SEEDS	SEASONING
Peanuts	Ground cinnamon
Pecans	Ground ginger
Hazelnuts	Ground black pepper
Sunflower seeds	Dried herbs (thyme, basil, lavender, etc.)
Pistachios	Cayenne pepper
Almonds	Ground nutmeg
Walnuts	Curry powder
Unsweetened coconut	Ground cloves
Sesame seeds	
Macadamia nuts	
Pumpkin seeds	

SEE IT IN A SLICE: *page 123*

» *Yields 2 cups chopped honeycomb candy*

½ cup granulated sugar

½ teaspoon kosher salt

¼ cup light corn syrup

1½ teaspoons baking soda

Honeycomb Candy

This stunning candy gets its signature web of air chambers from the addition of a large amount of baking soda relative to the quantity of sugar used in the recipe. The base recipe will bubble more than the variations, since corn syrup has less moisture than the other sweeteners.

1. Line a cookie sheet with greased parchment paper, foil, or a silicone baking mat.

2. In a sauce pan large enough to accommodate the mixture eventually growing 4 to 5 times its original size, combine the sugar, salt, and corn syrup. Cook over medium-high heat until it reaches hard crack consistency, or 300°F on a candy thermometer, about 10 minutes.

3. Remove the pan from the heat and immediately stir in the baking soda. The mixture will bubble up significantly. Stir just until combined, but not so much that you knock down the gorgeous foam that's forming. Pour onto the prepared cookie sheet.

4. Allow the honeycomb candy to cool completely before handling. Store in an airtight container in a cool, dry place for up to a week.

5. If using in a cake filling, finely chop the honeycomb candy and sprinkle onto a cake layer that's been topped with buttercream or another creamy filling.

HONEYCOMB CANDY VARIATIONS

Honey Honeycomb Candy	Replace the light corn syrup with ¼ cup honey.
Maple Honeycomb Candy	Replace 2 tablespoons of the light corn syrup with 2 tablespoons pure maple syrup.
Whiskey or Rum Honeycomb Candy	Reduce the light corn syrup to 2 tablespoons. In step 2, add 2 tablespoons whiskey or rum to the sugar mixture when it reaches a hard ball consistency, or 265°F on a candy thermometer.
Molasses Honeycomb Candy	Reduce the light corn syrup to 2 tablespoons. In step 2, add 2 tablespoons molasses to the sugar mixture when it reaches hard ball consistency, or 265°F on a candy thermometer.

Nut Butter Crunch

I went on a vision quest to find this recipe. As a pastry chef, drawing inspiration from candy bar flavors was an easy way to come up with a fancy dessert that everyone would crave. Snickers, Mounds, Reese's Peanut Butter Cups—those were all easy to replicate. But Butterfinger eluded me for quite some time. The day I added peanut butter instead of heavy cream to the end of the caramel candy-making process has gone down as a top-5 day for me. Kids, husband, house, Butterfinger.

1. Line a cookie sheet with heavy-duty aluminum foil and grease the foil with cooking spray.

2. In a medium saucepan, combine the syrup, water, and sugar. Cook over medium-high heat until the mixture reaches 300°F on a candy thermometer or the hard crack stage, 10 to 15 minutes.

3. Remove the pan from the heat and immediately whisk in the peanut butter. Pour onto the prepared cookie sheet and smooth the top with a heatproof rubber spatula.

4. Allow the nut butter crunch to cool completely before breaking into chunks or chopping. Store in an airtight container in a cool, dry place for up to a week.

5. If using as a cake filling, finely chop the nut butter crunch and sprinkle onto a cake layer that's been topped with buttercream or another creamy filling. Top the creamy, crunchy filling with another layer of cake.

SEE IT IN A SLICE: *page 127*

» *Yields 2 cups chopped nut butter crunch candy*

Cooking spray

⅔ cup Lyle's Golden Syrup (or corn syrup)

⅔ cup water

2 cups granulated sugar

2 cups smooth peanut butter

NUT BUTTER CRUNCH VARIATIONS ----------------

Hazelnut Butter Crunch	Substitute hazelnut paste for the peanut butter.
Sunflower Seed Butter Crunch	Substitute sunflower seed butter for the peanut butter.
Almond Nut Butter Crunch	Substitute almond butter for the peanut butter.

» *Yields 2 to 3 cups meringue*

3 large egg whites, room temperature

¾ cup granulated sugar

1 teaspoon pure vanilla extract

Meringue

Fancy French cakes are sometimes filled with a meringue layer called *dacquoise*. The meringue used to make traditional dacquoise is very similar in texture to a macaroon, with chopped nuts folded into the batter. Modern cakes employ meringue layers that are much more varied in fruit, chocolate, and citrus flavors, to name a few.

Macaroon-style batter can be very tricky. The batter and I do not always see eye to eye. It's my baking kryptonite. I would rather roll puff pastry all day for a week (well, maybe not that long), than be forced to pipe perfect macaroons for a minute. That's why I don't make traditional dacquoise when I want a meringue-y crunch in my cakes. This simple meringue may not be quite as refined, but once layered with other cakes, fillings, and buttercream, it takes on very similar qualities to its fancier counterpart.

You'll use the uncooked meringue to create the decorations for the Showers of Love Cake (page 175) and the Modern Meringue Cake (page 177).

➕ **DOCTOR, DOCTOR!** *Purchase meringue cookies at the supermarket or bakery. Chop them up to sprinkle within your cake's layers. Save some whole meringues for decorating the cake.*

MERINGUE VARIATIONS ─ ─ ─ ─ ─ ─ ─ ─ ─ ─ ─ ─ ─ ─ ─ ─ ─ ─

Nut Meringue	Fold ½ cup very finely chopped toasted nuts (assorted or a single kind) into the meringue at the end of step 2. At the same time, add 1 tablespoon of a corresponding flavored liqueur to enhance the nut flavor.
Chocolate Meringue	Add ¼ cup Dutch-processed cocoa powder into the whipping meringue after adding the sugar in step 2.
Citrus Meringue	Add 1 tablespoon grated citrus zest and 2 tablespoons citrus juice (assorted or a single kind) to the whipping meringue in step 2.
Berry Meringue	Add 2 tablespoons berry jam to the whipping meringue after adding the sugar in step 2.

**SEE IT IN
A SLICE:**
page 198

1. Position a rack in the center of the oven and preheat to 200°F. Line a cookie sheet with parchment paper.

2. Pour the egg whites into the clean, dry bowl of a stand mixer fitted with the paddle attachment (or a large metal bowl if using an electric hand mixer). Whip on medium-high speed until frothy. Continue to whip the whites while slowly pouring in the sugar and vanilla extract. Whip until the whites form stiff peaks, 5 to 7 minutes.

3. Transfer the meringue to a large piping bag. Snip the tip off the bag. Shape the meringues according to your specific project:

If using as a cake layer, first trace the outline of the cake pan that corresponds to the size of your cake layers onto the parchment paper with a black permanent marker. Flip the paper over onto the cookie sheet. Starting in the center of the circle, pipe concentric circles of meringue to fill in the circle.

If using as an element of crunch within cake layers, pipe long sticks of meringue at least 1 inch apart on the parchment-lined cookie sheet. Once cooled, chop the sticks into chunks and sprinkle onto a cake layer that's been topped with buttercream or another creamy filling.

4. Bake for 60 to 90 minutes, possibly longer depending on the humidity. Meringues are done when they are firm to the touch and no longer tacky. You should be able to easily lift them from the parchment paper without sticking.

5. Place the sheet on a rack to cool. But, if it's very humid or raining, turn off the oven when the cookies are done and leave them in there, with the door propped open, for another 20 to 30 minutes to continue drying out. There isn't any threat of overbaking meringues at this temperature. When in doubt, leave them in to dry out.

Odds are, if you're hot and sticky, your meringue will be, too. Humidity in the air can prevent meringue cookies from drying out as quickly as you'd like. If the weather's feeling tropical, kick back and enjoy another umbrella drink while the cookies take a little more time in the oven.

UNICORN
thought

Crunch Clusters

Both of these recipes, chocolate-coated and candy-coated, are wonderful ways to incorporate unique elements that are not typically found in layer cakes. Although any cookie, cereal, pretzel, or cracker will work with either recipe, sweet cookies and cereals tend to match better with a chocolate coating, and salty crackers and pretzels are better with the crisp, candy shell. Some work with all. Experiment to find your favorite combinations, or follow the chart on page 90 to find a great match.

**SEE IT IN
A SLICE:**
page 134

» *Yields a generous
2 cups clusters*

**8 ounces chocolate
(dark, milk, or
white)**

**2 cups cereal or
crushed cookies,
crackers, or
pretzels (see chart
on page 90)**

CHOCOLATE-COATED CLUSTERS

✚ **DOCTOR, DOCTOR!** *No time to temper? Use coating chocolate instead.*

1. Line a cookie sheet with parchment paper.

2. Place the chocolate in a heatproof bowl. Melt in the microwave on high for 30 seconds at a time, stirring between each interval, or melt in a double boiler. Temper the chocolate (see page 183) if you plan on using the clusters to garnish plates or decorate a cake. There's no need to temper if you're only going to use them inside the cake.

3. Add the cereal or crushed cookies to the melted chocolate. Stir to coat with a rubber spatula. Pour the coated mixture onto the prepared cookie sheet.

4. Allow the coated clusters to cool completely before breaking into chunks or chopping. Store in an airtight container in a cool, dry place for up to 2 weeks.

5. If using in a cake filling, finely chop the crunch clusters and sprinkle onto a cake layer that's been topped with buttercream or another creamy filling. Top the creamy, crunchy filling with another layer of cake.

CANDY-COATED CLUSTERS

SEE IT IN A SLICE: *page 203*

//

1. Line a cookie sheet with parchment paper.

2. In a small saucepan, combine the butter, brown sugar, and honey. Cook over medium-high heat until the mixture is golden and bubbly, 5 to 7 minutes.

3. Remove from the heat. Add the salt and crushed crackers or pretzels to the saucepan and stir to coat with a heatproof rubber spatula.

4. Pour the mixture onto the prepared cookie sheet. Using the rubber spatula, spread the pieces out into little clumps.

5. Allow the candy clusters to cool completely before breaking into chunks or chopping. Store in an airtight container in a cool, dry place for up to a week.

6. If using in a cake filling, finely chop the crunch clusters and sprinkle onto a cake layer that's been topped with buttercream or another creamy filling. Top the creamy, crunchy filling with another layer of cake.

» *Yields a generous 2 cups clusters*

2½ tablespoons butter

2½ tablespoons packed dark brown sugar

2½ tablespoons honey

¼ teaspoon salt

2 cups cereal or crushed crackers, pretzels, or cookies (see chart on page 90)

CRUNCH CLUSTER COMBINATIONS ------------

I've done some of the heavy lifting for you and tested endless crunch cluster combinations. Tough job, but someone had to do it. Find your cookie, cracker, or cereal on the left and look for the star under the coating(s) that pair best with it. For example, candy-coated Froot Loops? No, thank you. Froot Loops coated with dark, milk, or white chocolate? Party time.

	CANDY	DARK CHOCOLATE	MILK CHOCOLATE	WHITE CHOCOLATE
COOKIES				
Oreos		★	★	★
Chocolate chip cookies		★	★	★
Sugar cookies	★	★	★	★
Gingersnaps	★	★	★	★
Wafer cones	★	★	★	★
CEREAL				
Rice Krispies	★	★	★	★
Froot Loops		★	★	★
Cocoa Puffs		★	★	★
Cornflakes	★	★	★	
Cheerios	★	★	★	★
CRACKERS				
Ritz crackers	★	★	★	★
Graham crackers	★	★	★	★
Cheez-Its	★	★		
Saltines	★	★	★	
Matzo	★	★	★	★

PART 3

*eye
candy*

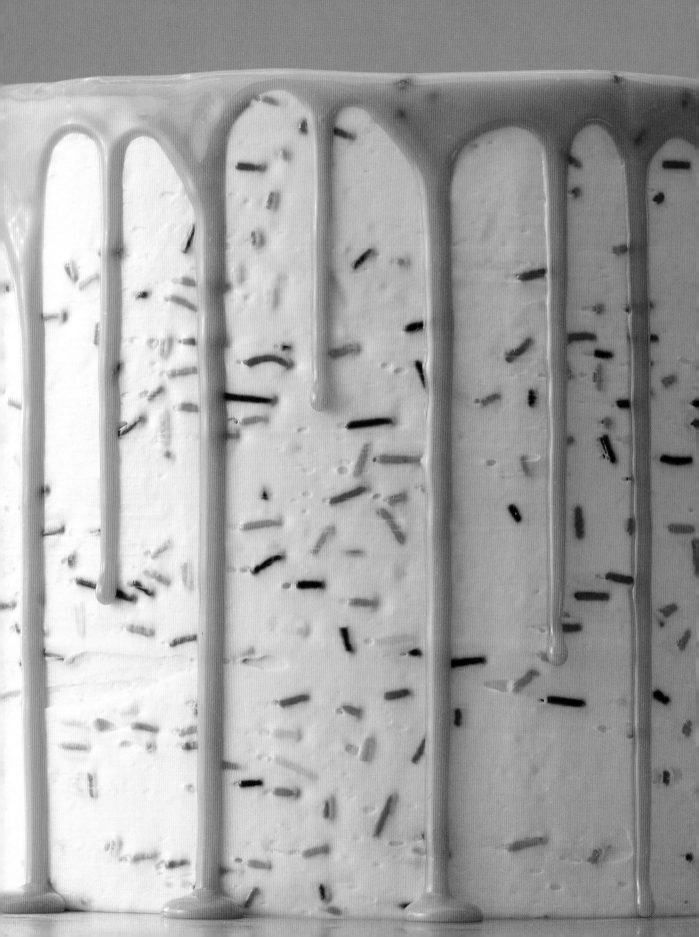

Chapter 6

....

ALL ABOUT THAT BASE

IF YOU WANT TO MAKE A PRETTY CAKE, YOU'VE GOT TO BE all about that base. No amount of decorating will save you if you start with a wonky, off-balance mess. A smooth, stable base cake is the best kind of canvas to showcase even the simplest decorations. Take the time to build a deliciously solid foundation, and you'll be rewarded with praise and adulation at your next big event.

For all of the finishes and cake projects in this section, use the buttercream that you like the best—Swiss Meringue (page 56), American (page 57), or Ermine (page 58).

HOW TO FILL A CAKE

1

Level
Use a serrated knife to level the domed top of the cake. Discard the dome or save it for snacking.

2

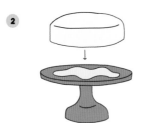

Smear a dollop of buttercream onto the center of your cake board or platter. Place the cake on the board and press down to adhere the cake to the board. Use the layer as-is and move on to step 5, or split the cake to create multiple layers.

3

Split
Eyeball it or use a ruler to find the center point of the edge of the cake. Mark that point with your knife.

4

Place one hand on top of the cake to steady it. Place your serrated knife on the center point and slice the cake in half with a smooth, sawing motion. Use the hand on top of the cake to spin it as you cut. Cut the cake all the way through.

5

Buttercream Filling
Apply a buttercream filling with an offset spatula or with a piping bag fitted with a large round tip.

6

Soft Fillings
For softer fillings (like jam, pastry cream, or ganache), first spread a crumb-coat-thin layer of buttercream over the surface of the cake to prevent the soft filling from soaking through. Pipe a "dam" of buttercream around the outer edges of the cake layer, then fill the ring with the soft filling.

7

Adding Crunch

Top the filling with a sprinkling of crunchy filling (optional).

8

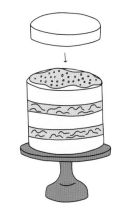

Adding more layers

Place the next layer of cake onto the filling, pressing down from the center toward the outer edges of the cake.

9

Repeat with as many layers as you like. Most of the cakes I make have 4 layers of cake and 3 layers of filling.

10

Pop the cake in the fridge for at least 30 minutes, or up to overnight, to allow the buttercream to firm up.

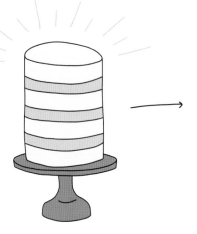

you did it!

HOW TO STACK A CAKE

1

Start with cakes that have been finished on cardboard cake rounds and thoroughly chilled.

2

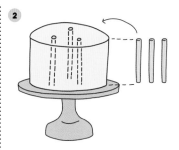

Measure and cut dowels the same height as the bottom tier of cake and insert them into the cake. Use three dowels if you're just stacking one tier on top. Increase the number of dowels you use in relation to how many tiers you're stacking and how large the cakes are. For example, if I am going to stack 6-inch, 8-inch, and 10-inch cakes, I place 5 dowels in the 10-inch cake below where the next tier will go and 3 dowels in the 8-inch cake below where the top tier will go.

3

Insert a smoothie straw into the center of the cake and pull it back out, removing a thin plug of cake. Leaving this tiny channel in the center of the cake gives air a place to go as your stacked cakes settle, preventing bubbles or bulges from forming on the sides of the cake. No need to do this with the top tier, just the cakes that will have others stacked on top of them.

4

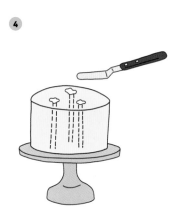

Spread a thin layer of buttercream over the tops of the dowels.

5

Use an offset spatula to help lift up the next tier of cake, placing it on top of the smeared buttercream and dowels. Press down lightly on the top of the cake to adhere it to the tier below. Repeat with more tiers as desired.

6

Fill the gap between tiers by piping a thin line of buttercream to cover the gap. Use a bench scraper to smooth over the piped line of buttercream, creating a seamless finish.

TIPS ON COLORING BUTTERCREAM

Pastels

Just a dab of color will do. Instead of squeezing the food coloring directly into your buttercream, dip a toothpick into the bottle and add the color to your buttercream a little at a time. Aim for a slightly lighter shade than what you're going for, as the color will continue to deepen over time.

Brights

If you don't have time to order a specific ultra-bright or neon color, try brightening up a shade by adding a drop or two of one of the lighter colors contained within your color. That sounds confusing, but in practice, it's not. For example, to turn leaf-green to lime-green, add a drop or two of yellow. (Yellow + blue = green; yellow is brighter than blue.) To make a coral-y orange, add a drop or two of yellow. For fuchsia, add red or pink to a purple base color. If you want to brighten a primary color, try adding a drop or two of white and/or the teensiest amount of yellow.

Dustys

I call these Martha Stewart colors. Olive, mauve, and slate are all good examples. Start with a bright gel color and muddle the tone by adding a little black, one drop at a time. If you're close, step away and allow the color to develop for an hour or so before adding more black.

Red

Achieve a bright, truly red buttercream that also doesn't taste like tin by planning ahead and using the right product for the job. Americolor Super Red or Tulip Red gel colors are my favorite options. Wilton's Red-Red and Christmas Red also work well and may be easier to find. Plan on adding about ½ teaspoon of color for every cup of buttercream. Start the coloring process the day before and let the buttercream chill in the fridge overnight to give the color time to develop. To further deepen red tones, add a drop or two of black.

Black

If you've ever tried to make black buttercream and ended up with something resembling a lavender-gray blob, you're not alone! The secret to truly black buttercream is to start with chocolate. You'll end up adding far less food coloring to achieve a solid shade. Just like red, start the process the day before to allow the color to reach its full potential.

True White

Crisp, white-as-snow buttercream can be made by using an all-shortening recipe. To brighten up a real buttercream made with the good stuff, add the absolute tiniest amount of violet food coloring to the batch. The brand isn't as important as the specific color—violet. The tiny drop should be about the same size as the tip of a toothpick. Use great restraint when adding the color; you can always add more. It might seem strange to add violet coloring to make frosting white, but the small amount of purple helps to counteract the yellow tint from the butter.

BUTTERCREAM AND GANACHE FINISHES

SMOOTH FINISHES

Smooth cakes are king in the cake world. They're a thing of beauty on their own, or the perfect clean canvas for any cake design. There are a number of techniques for achieving a smooth buttercream or ganache finish that involve things like acrylic disks, flipping cakes upside down, and other sorts of cake gymnastics. If you are entering a cake smoothing contest, then I suggest you seek out one of those methods. If you are interested in a smooth-enough cake without the hassle, kick it old-school with me and my trusty bench scraper.

When left in a bowl covered with plastic wrap at room temperature for 4 to 6 hours (or up to overnight), ganache becomes similar in consistency to buttercream. Follow the same steps to slather on a smooth or textured ganache cake finish. (See recipe on page 62.)

1. Use an icing spatula to cover your cake in a thin layer, or crumb coat, of buttercream. Pop the cake in the fridge until the layer has set up firm, about 30 minutes.

2. Place the crumb-coated cake on a turntable. Pile a mound of buttercream on top of the cake. Use the icing spatula to flatten the mound while spreading buttercream out and over the edges of the cake. Spin the cake on the stand while holding the spatula steady on top of the cake.

3. Apply a thick layer of buttercream, covering all the way around the sides of the cake and up to the top edge.

4. Hold a bench scraper so that the long, flat edge is vertical against the side of the cake. Keep the scraper still while you spin the turntable. The buttercream will start to smooth out and collect on the bench scraper. Stop and wipe the buttercream back into the bowl every few turns.

5. Smooth the top by holding the long, flat edge of the offset spatula or bench scraper horizontally above the top edge of the cake. Pull back, up, and away in a smooth, confident motion. Spin the cake and repeat all along the edges until smooth enough.

6. Serve right away, or chill the cake to firm up the smooth finish or before adding additional decorative details.

Ombré Finish

1. Start with a crumb-coated cake.

2. Fill large piping bags with buttercream in your desired shades of color (or different shades of thick ganache).

3. Snip the tips off the bags. Starting with the color you'd like to have on the bottom of the cake, pipe lines of that color all around the sides of the cake, up as far as you'd like that color to reach. Repeat until the cake is completely covered, using the colors of your choice.

4. Repeat steps 4 through 6 for Smooth Finishes above.

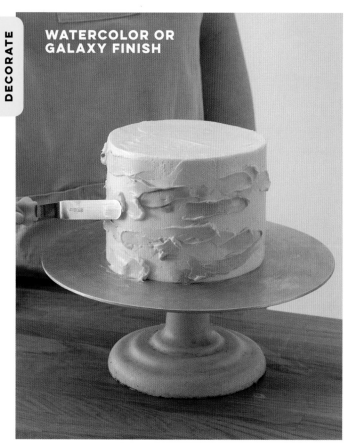

WATERCOLOR OR GALAXY FINISH

DRIPPED GANACHE FINISH

Watercolor or Galaxy Finish

1. Start with a smooth solid or ombré finish (see page 100).

2. Apply blotches of colored buttercream in various shades all around the sides of the cake.

3. Use the bench scraper to smooth and spread the blotches, blending them into the rest of the buttercream finish.

4. To create a galaxy effect, start with a solid black finish and smooth on blotches of purple, blue, and yellow.

POURED GANACHE FINISHES

1. Start with a thoroughly chilled crumb-coated cake. Pouring warm ganache over a room-temperature cake will cause the edges to soften.

2. Place a drip rack or cooling rack onto a rimmed cookie sheet. Set the chilled cake on the rack.

3. Using a ladle or spouted glass measuring cup, pour freshly made ganache over the top of the cake, starting at the center. Continue pouring, letting the hot ganache run over the sides of the cake, until the entire cake is coated. Allow the cake to cool to room temperature before moving, 15 to 20 minutes. Approximately 3 cups of ganache will cover a 6-inch round layer cake.

4. Slide a chef's knife or offset spatula under the cake to clear away any drips that may have hardened on the bottom edge of the cake.

5. Scrape up and save the extra ganache left behind on the rimmed baking sheet.

DRIPPED GANACHE FINISHES

1. Start with a cake that's been thoroughly chilled. The drip can be done on a cake at any stage (naked, crumb-coated, finished), depending on the look you're going for. Set the cake on a stand or platter, or on a cooling rack for easier cleanup.

2. Pour a cup or so of warm ganache into a piping bag or plastic squeeze bottle. For the perfect drip, ganache should be a runny consistency. Snip the tip off the bag and squirt drips of ganache over the edge of your cake in random spots.

3. Once you have the desired look on the sides of your cake, fill in the top with more ganache using a spoon or ladle. Pour a small amount on the top of the cake and use the rounded bottom of the spoon to push the ganache toward the edges of the cake until it is covered.

TEXTURED FINISHES

Encrusted Finishes

Sprinkles, Sanding Sugar, Chopped Nuts, Coconut

1. Start with a smooth buttercream finish.

2. Place your turntable on a rimmed cookie sheet to catch sprinkles as they fall.

3. Scoop up a handful of sprinkles (or sugar, nuts, or coconut) and press the sprinkles into the sides of the cake. Spin the turntable and repeat until the entire surface is covered.

4. If you'd like to create areas of relief (stripes, dots, etc.) within an encrusted finish, you'll need to first cut the shape you want to make out of parchment paper, then grease one side of the paper with shortening and smooth it onto the side of your chilled cake, greased side down. Continue with step 3. Pop the cake back in the fridge until firm, 10 to 15 minutes. Use the tip of a paring knife to carefully lift away the pieces of parchment paper.

Speckled Finishes

Chocolate, Sprinkles

1. Fold 1 cup finely chopped chocolate or sprinkles into one batch of buttercream.

2. Use the speckled buttercream to finish your cake, following the steps in Smooth Finishes.

3. Further enhance your speckled finish by adding more chopped chocolate or sprinkles, following the Encrusted Finishes directions above.

Rustic Finishes

1. Create a fluffy rustic look by using the back of a spoon to apply swishy swirls all over the buttercream. **A**

2. Make a cross-hatch pattern by dragging the tines of a fork through the buttercream. **B**

3. Drag the tip of an icing spatula or spoon through the buttercream to create vertical or horizontal stripes. **C**

Piped Finishes

1. For textured stripes, pipe vertical lines all around the edges of the cake using a star tip. **D**

2. For a pressed petal look, pipe vertical rows of dots with a round or star tip on the side. Spread the dots out with the tip of an icing spatula. Repeat all around the sides of the cake, overlapping dots as you go. **F**

3. Pipe ruffles using a leaf (pictured) or star tip. Hold the tip over the surface of the cake and wiggle it back and forth while piping rows, vertically or horizontally. **E**

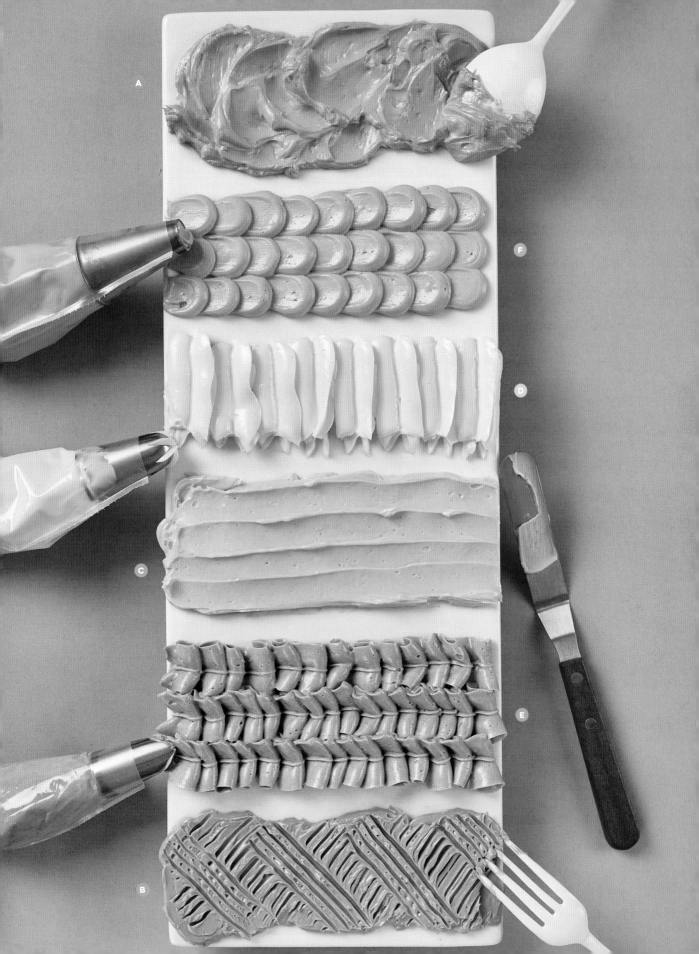

NAKED FINISH

» Grease your pans so they're nice and slick! Without frosting or fondant to hide any baking imperfections, you'll need those beauties to slide out of their pans in one piece.

» Distribute batter evenly among your cake pans to make your job easier when it's time to cut and fill.

» To keep your naked cake looking straight and beautiful, take the time to measure your cakes before cutting. Even layers don't only look beautiful, they also add stability to your finished cake.

» Fresh is best. Naked cakes leave much of the cake surface exposed to air, which can lead to the cake drying out more quickly. Schedule your baking as close to the event as possible.

» Choose stable cakes and fillings—think pound cake, birthday cake, and frostings that set firm like ganache, AMBC, or SMBC. Add fresh fruit shortly before serving.

» Use a piping bag when filling your cake to keep layers even and to prevent your filling from marking up the sides of your cake. When piping your filling, give yourself a little lip (about ¼-inch) to allow for it to spread a little when the other cake layers are added on top.

» For a semi-naked cake, apply a crumb coat to the exterior of the cake that's thicker than a normal crumb coat, but thin enough that streaks of cake show through.

» Chill out, man. After all that hard work to keep your cakes and fillings clean and straight, give your naked cake some time to chill in the fridge before moving or serving.

PROJECT REMIX

All of the decorating techniques in this book are demonstrated on beautiful, tall layer cakes—the supermodels of the cake world. Please don't let this make your cupcakes or one-tier wonder feel inadequate. All cakes are beautiful and deserve chic and fun finishing touches. When flipping through these project pages, keep in mind that most, if not all, of the techniques shown will also look fabulous on top of a sheet cake, a shorter cake, or as cupcake toppers.

Chapter 7

··································

CANDY

HEAD STRAIGHT TO THE CAKE PROJECTS IN THIS CHAPTER when you need a cute cake on the fly. The candy cake projects are the easiest and the quickest to pull together, with the exception of the Candied Mandala Cake. That cake explores the "candy" idea in a new way, using thinly-sliced fruits and veggies. It's a great introduction to the pastry-inspired techniques in the chapters to follow.

CANDY CAKES 101

Decorating cakes with store-bought candy is a simple, inexpensive way to customize a cake you baked yourself or one that rode in the cart while you headed for the candy aisle. Candy-coated designs aren't just for the kiddies, either. Taking a new look at time-saving shortcuts can yield surprisingly chic results.

Tips for Handling and Storing Candy

» Hard candy decorations can be made well in advance and stored in an airtight container until the candy's expiration date.

» When gummy candy has been melted and reshaped, it can become tougher than the original piece of candy. It will also dry out and harden faster than candy straight from the bag. Store gummy candy decorations in an airtight container for up to a week.

» Candied fruit and vegetable petals are sensitive to humidity and heat. They can be made a day in advance and stored in an airtight container at room temperature.

» Store candy in a cool, dark, dry place. Only refrigerate candy that specifically states it on the label.

» Apply candy designs shortly before presenting and serving your cake. The humidity in your refrigerator can cause the color to run in hard, gummy, or chewy candies.

» When working with melted candy, always keep a bowl of cold water nearby just in case a drop or two gets on your skin. Submerge the affected area into the cold water as quickly as possible. The sooner you cool the hot sugar, the less likely your burn will blister.

» Greasing the blade of your knife with a thin coating of shortening will make life easier when cutting anything that's sticky or gummy.

» Wipe your knife as you go to prevent the blade from getting gunked up.

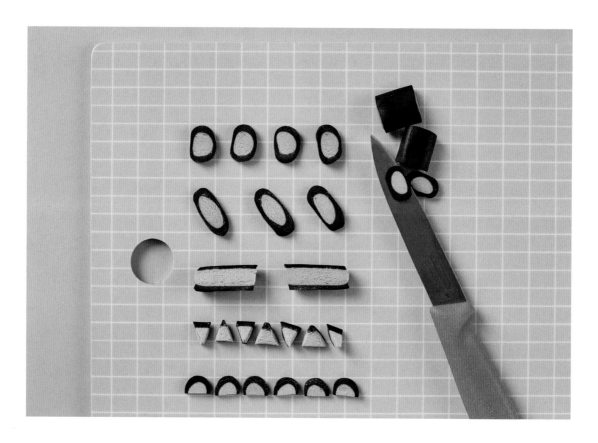

Allsorts of Order Cake

A great trick for elevating ordinary decorative elements is to simply line them up. Create lines, rows, grids, and other patterns with whole or cut pieces of candy.

You may think that the bride is the toughest customer in all of cake making, but you'd be wrong. Brides are easy once you learn to speak their language (rustic chic, modern preppy, simple elegance). The most challenging cakes to design are for teens and tweens. Can't be too cutesie, even though they still think dinosaurs and superheroes are cool. Get into the later teenage years and I know what they're interested in, but that's not exactly appropriate for a cake they're going to share with Grandma. Harnessing the power of candy patterns will enable you to create modern cake designs that appeal to all.

Licorice allsorts are a colorful candy blend that we have the Brits to thank for. They can be found online or in finer candy shops. Use your favorite candy assortment if you can't locate them in your area or if you're not a fan of licorice.

😎 **FAUX FABULOUS:** *Cut down on cutting time. Choose one candy to work with and use it to create a single repeating design.*

///

STEP 1: Cut a black and white licorice cylinder into thin slices. Alternate cut pieces and whole cylinders to create a border along the bottom edge of the cake. Cut more licorice slices as needed.

STEP 2: Slice black, white, and pink licorice squares into thin pieces. Line up the pieces in a grid pattern.

STEP 3: Cut yellow and pink licorice rounds into thin slices. Arrange them in lines, alternating colors with each row.

STEP 4: Slice some of the blue nonpareil-coated licorice rounds in half. Place the cut rounds, sticky-side down, onto the cake in a simple diamond pattern.

→

6-inch round layer cake, finished with blue buttercream speckled with black and white sprinkles (see page 104)

Licorice allsorts (or your favorite candy blend)

Small sharp knife

UNICORN thought

Grease the blade of your knife with vegetable shortening to keep yourself from getting into all sorts of a sticky mess.

CAKEQUATION

ESPRESSO BIRTHDAY CAKE
(page 34)

+

SALTED CARAMEL BUTTERCREAM
(page 60)

+

TOFFEE
(page 81)

ALLSORTS OF ORDER CAKE

6-inch round layer cake, finished in raspberry buttercream or vanilla buttercream tinted pink

Layered chewy taffy candy or filled licorice sticks (like Hi-Chew)

Cream-filled licorice bites (flower-shaped)

Green and pink taffy

Gummy peaches

Tiny yellow crunchy candies

Parchment paper

Small sharp knife

Sweet Bouquet Cake

I'd like to say there's some sort of romantic, inspirational story behind the design of this cake, but there isn't. I saw a lamp. I thought the lamp looked like candy. I turned it into a cake. A candy-covered cake worthy of a sophisticated soiree.

The real story here is how to make $10 worth of drugstore candy look like a million bucks. To take candy from kiddie to chic, think outside the box. More specifically, grab a knife and get cutting. Explore what the insides of different candies look like. Discover what they look like cut in half or thirds or into tiny pieces. Combine these new shapes to mimic floral patterns from wallpaper, fabric or, in my case, a lampshade. Consider this list of candy a general outline. Get creative and use whatever is available near you.

😎 **FAUX FABULOUS:** *Skip all the knife work and create a simpler floral arrangement using premade gummy flowers and leaves.*

Large Open Flowers

STEP 1: Cut thin slices of layered taffy candy at an angle. I made two of these flowers on the cake, one using pink candy with white centers and the other using yellow candy with white centers, but you can use whatever colors you like. As you go, separate the cut pieces and spread them out on parchment paper so that they don't stick together. Cut three to four pieces in half to form little triangles.

STEP 2: Place a line of five or so cut candy pieces onto the cake. This is the top row of the front of the flower. Layer another row of cut candy pieces so that the tips of this next row overlap the first. Continue layering pieces of candy to create the shape of the flower.

STEP 3: Press a semicircle of tiny yellow crunchy candies into the buttercream just above the first row of petals. Fill in the spaces between the petals with candy. Add a few of the cut triangles around the top edge of the semicircle.

Fern Leaves

STEP 1: Cut thin slices of layered green taffy candy at an angle, just as you made the petals in step 1 for the large open flowers.

STEP 2: Place a line of cut slices onto the cake in a row at a slight angle. Add a second row, mirroring the first, to create a shape similar to a fern leaf.

Flat Leaves

STEP 1: Roll a piece of green taffy between two pieces of parchment paper. Microwave the candy for 5 seconds to soften, if needed.

STEP 2: Use a small knife or leaf cookie cutter to cut leaf shapes from the taffy. Pinch the pointed ends to give the leaves shape.

Flat Open Rose

STEP 1: Cut thin slices of layered taffy candy at an angle, the same as in step 1 for the large open flowers and leaves. I used white candy with an orange center, but you can use whatever colors you like.

STEP 2: Place one of the tiny end slices onto the cake as the center of the rose. Add more pieces of candy, ascending in size, around the center piece.

Large Peach Rose

STEP 1: Gummy peaches are flat, triangular-shaped pieces of candy. Cut all three sides off the triangle and discard (or enjoy!) the center. Repeat with two more gummy peaches.

STEP 2: Place two of the cut strips onto the cake, cut-side down (like two Cs facing each other), to form the center of the flower. Add more strips around the first two, slightly cupped toward the center of the flower.

Small Roses

STEP 1: Roll a piece of pink taffy between two pieces of parchment paper. Microwave the candy for 5 seconds to soften, if needed.

STEP 2: Cut the candy into ½-inch-wide strips. Coil one of the strips up and pinch the bottom to give the coil a tapered shape. Repeat with more strips to make more tiny coiled flowers.

Tiny Blossom Clusters

Cut a cream-filled licorice flower into thin slices. Arrange the slices on the cake in clusters, mimicking hydrangea or hyacinth plants.

All Together Now

Add the larger flowers to your cake first, and then use the smaller blossoms and leaves to fill in around them. Follow my lead and assemble a crescent-shaped arrangement on the top of your cake, build a candy garden around the sides, or create a dramatic all-over floral design.

Avoid a sticky situation by lightly greasing the blade of your knife with shortening before cutting the candy. Wipe and re-grease the blade as needed.

UNICORN thought

CAKEQUATION

GINGER BIRTHDAY CAKE
(page 34)

+

PINEAPPLE LIME JAM
(page 70)

+

CANDIED MACADAMIA NUT CRUNCH
(page 80)

+

RASPBERRY BUTTERCREAM
(page 61)

SWEET BOUQUET CAKE

Winter Village Cake

Where do teeny-tiny gingerbread men live? In teeny-tiny cookie houses, of course! I've made these itty-bitty wafer cookie houses for many different occasions, but the original source of inspiration came from an article I read about a forest in England. Forest keepers were complaining about the number of fairy doors popping up on trees. At times, up to 20 doors would appear on a single tree. It was, perhaps, the most adorable problem of all-time. I, being the solutions-oriented person that I am, went straight to work on creating more affordable fairy housing. At less than a dollar per house, these revolutionary tiny homes grew to serve more than just the fairy population. Leprechauns, tiny puppies and kitties, chickies and bunnies, and now gingerbread men can be proud to call a mini wafer cookie house home.

😎 **FAUX FABULOUS:** *Too much hustle and bustle in your holiday season? Pick up a few mini gingerbread kits at the craft store. Build one for the top of the cake and use the rest of the premade panels to finish the sides.*

Houses

STEP 1: Using the pattern on the cookie as your guide, cut one of the wafer cookies in half on a diagonal. Trim the other side of the wafer to match, creating the peak of the gingerbread-house roof.

STEP 2: Flip the other side of the cookie around and line up the bottom with the base of the roof. Trim the piece into a square. This square will become the side walls of the house.

STEP 3: Stand up both wafer cookie pieces and cut them down the middle, leaving two peaked walls and two side walls.

STEP 4: Melt the white coating chocolate. Dip one side of a square into the melted chocolate and attach it to the back of one of the peaked panels. Repeat with the other square and attach it to the other side of the same peaked panel. Let the chocolate harden (about 5 minutes) before picking up the assembled piece and dipping the open ends of the walls into the melted chocolate. Attach the peaked back panel. Set the house aside until the chocolate has hardened completely, about 5 minutes.

6-inch round layer cake, finished with sky blue buttercream (see page 99)

Additional 2 cups buttercream, in a piping bag fitted with a large round tip

2 cups white coating chocolate or white chocolate

Neapolitan wafer cookies

Gingerbread men confetti quins

Round confetti quins

Candy cane confetti quins

Snowflake confetti quins

White nonpareils

White sugar pearls

Candy-coated licorice sticks

Jelly beans

Green, white, and pink taffy sticks

Small sharp knife

Find tips for working with chocolate and coating chocolate on page 182.

STEP 5: Cut small pieces of the taffy stick to create a roof for your teeny-tiny little wafer cookie house. Pinch the pieces together at the peak so that the roof doesn't slide off.

STEP 6: Use the small knife to trim off the end of a yellow jelly bean. Stand up the jelly bean on the cut end and trim off the front and back of the bean. Attach it to the front of the house with a dab of melted chocolate.

Have fun decorating your itsy-bitsy teeny-weeny wafer cookie house with more confetti quins and nonpareils.

STEP 7: Repeat step 1 to make the flat house panels for the side of the cake. Cut the differently colored wafers at varying heights. Decorate the wafers with jelly beans and confetti quins. Repeat step 5, but with much thinner strips of taffy to make little roofs for the panels.

Snowman

STEP 1: Line up three candy pearls in a row and attach them to each other using the melted white coating chocolate. Allow the chocolate to harden, about 5 minutes, before adding the hat.

STEP 2: To make the hat, trim off the end of a black jelly bean. Cut a thin slice from the center of the jelly bean to make the brim. Stick the slice on top of the stack of candy pearls and top it with the domed end of the jelly bean.

All Together Now

Cover the top of the cake with piped mounds and dollops of vanilla buttercream. Nestle the little gingerbread house and a petite snowman into one of the buttercream hills. Introduce a few teeny-tiny gingerbread man sprinkles to their new abode. Create a village scene around the sides of the cake with the flat house panels, snowmen, sprinkle quins, and nonpareils. Fill the sky with a flurry of snowflake sprinkles.

CAKEQUATION

GINGERBREAD POUND CAKE
(page 42)

➕

CINNAMON BUTTERCREAM
(page 61)

➕

PISTACHIO BRITTLE
(page 82)

WINTER VILLAGE CAKE

Queen Bee Cake

The design of this cake is a nod to one of my earliest and most popular wedding cake designs, the Napoleonic Bee Cake. It was the very first cake of mine to appear on *The Cake Blog*, as well as numerous other blogs, websites, and bridal magazines. I created the repeating hexagonal design over the entire surface of a three-tier cake with just a single hexagon cutter. Now, there are tools available to make the process much quicker, like silicone texture mats and specialty cutters.

This updated and simplified version of that design would make an adorably chic birthday cake for a girl who runs the world or a romantic anniversary cake your bae will love like XO.

//

Position a rack in the center of the oven and preheat to 275°F.

STEP 1: Unwrap the hard candies and separate them by color into zip-top bags. Push all the air out of the bags before sealing them. It's important that you specifically use freezer bags, because the plastic is thicker and will hold up better to all of the smashing.

Place a bag of candy on top of a dish towel. Fold the towel up and over the bag of candy. This helps to protect your countertop and eyes, should any candy escape the bag. Grab the rolling pin and whack that bag like your boo just called Becky with the good hair. Crush the candy into small pieces. Repeat with the other bag.

STEP 2: Place the hexagon cookie cutters on a parchment-lined cookie sheet. Lightly spray the cutters with cooking spray. Fill half of the cutters with crushed yellow candy. Don't be too tidy with the job; the end result will be more interesting if you allow a few pieces to go astray into other cutters. Fill the other half of the cutters with crushed orange candy the same way.

STEP 3: Place the tray in the oven to melt the candy into solid shapes, about 7 minutes. Remove the tray from the oven and set aside until the cutters are cool enough to handle, about 5 minutes.

STEP 4: Carefully push the hard candy pieces out of the cutters. Repeat to make more hexagons.

→

6-inch round layer cake, finished in orange, yellow, and white ombré buttercream (see page 100)

1 set hexagonal cookie cutters

Orange and yellow hard candies

1 cup yellow coating chocolate

Gold Jordan almonds

Gold Sixlets

Gold pearls

Sliced almonds

Zip-top freezer bags

Rolling pin

Cooking spray

Parchment paper

Dish towel

Find tips for working with chocolate and coating chocolate on page 182.

Queen Bees

STEP 1: Melt the yellow coating chocolate. Dip a gold Sixlet into the melted candy and stick it to the thin end of a Jordan almond. Dip a gold pearl into the melted candy and stick it on top of the Sixlet to complete the bee's body.

STEP 2: Layer two almond slices on top of each other. Dip one end of the stack into the melted candy and slide it under the bee's body where the Sixlet meets the sugar pearl. Repeat with another set of wings on the other side. Repeat to make more bees. Allow the chocolate to harden completely before using the bees on the cake, about 10 minutes.

All Together Now

Arrange the candy hexagons on the cake so that the color looks like it's moving from yellow to orange across the cake. Complete the look with a swarm of queen bees.

UNICORN thought

Think you're ready for this jelly? Create a similar look by melting chopped-up yellow and orange gummy candies.

CAKEQUATION

HONEY POUND CAKE
(page 42)

LEMON CURD
(page 65)

WHISKEY HONEYCOMB CANDY
(page 84)

HONEY BUTTERCREAM
(page 60)

QUEEN BEE CAKE

Poppy Pops Cake

If you're ever in need of a muse, one of the first places to turn for cake design inspiration is fashion. I can't tell you how many times I've stopped and taken a quick picture of a necklace, shoes, dress, etc., because I saw it and thought, "OOOH! That could be cool on a cake." Cake trends and fashion trends run hand-in-hand. Ruffles, lace, pearls, florals, and animal prints are just a few shared design themes. The inspiration for this cake design came from an Oscar de la Renta gown that Sarah Jessica Parker wore to the Met Gala in 2014. I jumped out of my seat when I saw that grid-patterned black and white train and actually took a picture of the TV, like the big cake dork that I am. Later, I just used that little thing called the Internet to look at the dozens of paparazzi shots from the event.

//

Position a rack in the center of the oven and preheat to 275°F.

STEP 1: Unwrap the hard candies and place them in a zip-top bag. Push all the air out of the bag before sealing. It's important that you specifically use a freezer bag, because the plastic is thicker and will hold up better to all of the smashing.

Place the bag of candy on top of a dish towel. Fold the towel up and over the bag to save your countertop and loved ones from any candy that should escape. Use the rolling pin to smash the candy into tiny chunks.

STEP 2: Tear off three 4-inch-wide sheets of foil and rip them into squares. Place one of the foil squares on a cookie sheet and spray it with a light coating of cooking spray. Pour about ¼ cup of smashed candy onto the foil and arrange the pieces into a circle that's 2 to 3 inches in diameter. Repeat this step five times, making six circles total.

→

6-inch round layer cake, finished with white buttercream (see page 99)

Red hard candy (like Jolly Ranchers or Life Savers)

Blackberry gumdrops (the kind coated with black nonpareils)

Mini dark chocolate squares

Heavy-duty aluminum foil

Large piping tips (doesn't matter what kind)

Zip-top freezer bag

Cutting board

Dish towel

Rolling pin

STEP 3: Place the tray in the oven to melt the candy into solid shapes, about 7 minutes. While the candy is in the oven, line up six large piping tips on a cutting board. Use a dish towel to steady them, if needed. Remove the cookie sheet from the oven. Working quickly but carefully, pick up the foil by the edges (the foil cools almost immediately) and drape the melted candy round over the top of a piping tip, foil-side down. Pull on the edges of the foil to get the shape you want. Repeat with the rest of the rounds. If any candy hardens, return the tray to the oven for a few seconds to re-soften. Allow the flowers to cool completely before using them on the cake, about 10 minutes.

UNICORN
thought

Feeling invincible? Instead of making six smaller flowers, make one gorgeous, oversized bloom for the top of your cake. Melt a large round of candy and drape it over an upside-down bowl to shape. Finish the center with a dark chocolate peppermint disk.

All Together Now

Flip over each flower and peel away the foil. Place the flowers on the top of the cake around the outer edge. Place a blackberry gumdrop in the center of each flower. Decorate the sides of the cake with rows of mini dark chocolate squares. The ones I used came individually wrapped in a bag and have a little ridge on the front. Place the squares onto the cake with the flat side facing out.

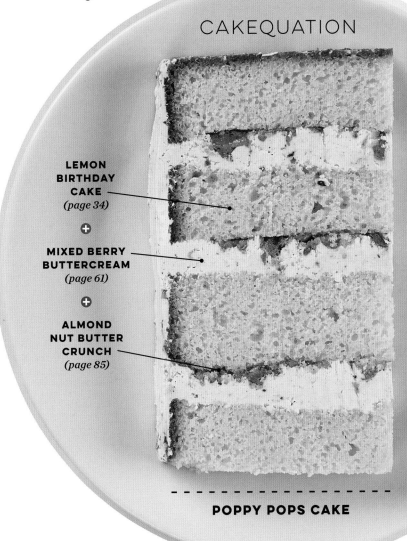

CAKEQUATION

LEMON BIRTHDAY CAKE
(page 34)

➕

MIXED BERRY BUTTERCREAM
(page 61)

➕

ALMOND NUT BUTTER CRUNCH
(page 85)

POPPY POPS CAKE

Over the Rainbow Cake

This wouldn't be my book if there wasn't at least one rainbow cake in it. Add in candy, a little calculated risk, and a few *Wizard of Oz* references and you basically have me as a cake.

Pulled sugar is the most fancy-pants skill in a pastry chef's toolbox. It takes years and years of practice and blisters to master. Isomalt is the medium of choice when a pastry chef wants to create a sugar garnish or figure that will hold its shape and maintain a beautiful, translucent shine. Lucky for us, store-bought sweets contain these same properties. Shaping crushed hard candies is a fun and relatively easy way to mimic the high-end look of sugar work.

//

Position a rack in the center of the oven and preheat to 275°F.

STEP 1: Unwrap the rainbow candies and group them by color.

STEP 2: Tear off a 5-inch-wide piece of foil and place it on a cookie sheet. Grease the foil with a light coating of cooking spray. Arrange the candy in tight rows on the foil. Fold the sides of the foil up along either side of the candy rainbow.

→

6-inch round layer cake, finished with a sky blue and white watercolor buttercream finish (see page 103)

Red, green, blue, and purple hard candy (like Jolly Ranchers)

Additional 2 cups vanilla buttercream, in a piping bag fitted with a large round tip

1 cup white nonpareils

Dish towel

Heavy-duty aluminum foil

Cooking spray

Ruler

4-inch round cake pan or something similarly shaped, to mold the rainbow

The interior of this cake is as much a part of the design as the exterior. Inside, black and white cake layers with a crunchy, almond yellow brick road make way for an outside of blue skies over the rainbow—just like in the movie, when Dorothy steps through the door of her grayscale life into the Technicolor world of Munchkinland.

UNICORN thought

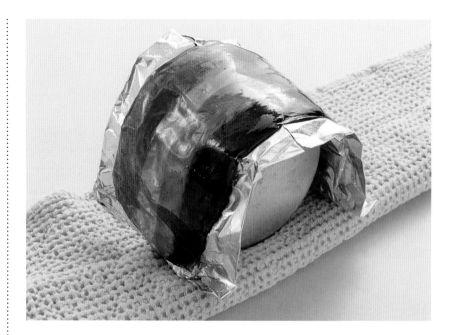

STEP 3: Place the tray in the oven to melt the candy into a solid shape, about 7 minutes. While the candy is in the oven, place the round cake pan (or something similar) on its side on top of a dish towel to steady it. Remove the tray from the oven. Allow the candy to cool for just a few minutes, until it's no longer so hot that it's runny. While the candy is still warm and pliable, lift up the foil and drape the rainbow over the cake pan. Unfold the edges of the foil or snip them with scissors so the foil lays flat. Pull down on the ends of the foil to shape it. Foil cools almost instantly, so you should be able to do this with your bare hands. If you're not comfortable with that, just keep the oven mitts on. Leave the rainbow on the cake pan until it has hardened completely, 5 to 10 minutes.

UNICORN thought

If shaping melted candy terrifies you, don't stress. Melt the candy in a classic arched rainbow shape. Lay the rainbow on flat or stand it up on top of the cake.

All Together Now

Carefully lift the rainbow off the cake pan and peel away the foil. Place the rainbow on top of the cake. Use a piping bag filled with vanilla buttercream to pipe clouds at the base of each end of the rainbow. Sprinkle the clouds with white nonpareils.

CAKEQUATION

BLACK VELVET BIRTHDAY CAKE *(page 38)*

+

VANILLA BIRTHDAY CAKE *(page 32)*

+

ALMOND TOFFEE *(page 81)*

+

YOUR FAVORITE VANILLA BUTTERCREAM *(page 55)*

+

CHOCOLATE CARAMEL *(page 75)*

- - - - - - - - - - - - - - - -

OVER THE RAINBOW CAKE

Chewable Planets Cake

I dreamt up these gummy planets a few years ago as a Valentine's Day treat for my son, Maxwell. When a subject piques his interest, he goes all in. We have planet shirts, inflatable planet beach balls, and even planet dinner plates. So it made perfect sense to present my little space cadet with a galaxy of gummies as a Valentine's treat. He's since moved on to exploring human anatomy, but gummy guts and brains are a little less appetizing. Unless you're a zombie, of course. I'm sure that'll be next.

///

Position a rack in the center of the oven and preheat to 275°F.

STEP 1: Tear off a piece of foil that's 1 inch larger all around than the round item you're going to use to make your planet mold. Search for circular items in different sizes to make the planets as accurate as possible. (Although I won't report you to NASA if you make them all the same size.)

Place a glass or round cookie cutter on the piece of foil. Press the edges of the foil over the bottom of the glass or cutter, making sure the sides are very tight and smooth. Repeat, making enough molds for all of your planets and a sun. Shape a little flat-bottomed foil boat for making Saturn's rings. Place all of your molds onto a cookie sheet and spray them with cooking spray.

STEP 2: Cut the gummy bears into strips and chunks and arrange them in the cups to create each planet's distinct color patterns. Keep the colors as close to reality as possible, but keep in mind that we are dealing with gummy bears here.

STEP 3: Put the cookie sheet in the oven to melt the gummy bears, 5 to 8 minutes. Check your planets at the 5-minute mark and pull out any that look done to you. Orange and yellow seem to melt much quicker than green, blue, and white. Use a toothpick or skewer to swirl the colors of the gas giants while the candy is still hot.

STEP 4: Allow the planets to cool on the cookie sheet for about 5 minutes. Move them to a plate and pop them into the fridge until

→

8-inch round layer cake, finished with a buttercream galaxy finish (see page 103)

1 cup white buttercream (see page 99)

1 cup gray coating chocolate

Red, orange, yellow, green, blue, purple, and white gummy bears

Heavy-duty aluminum foil

Cooking spray

Small sharp knife

Toothpick or skewer

Round cookie cutters or drinking glasses (anything small and round)

Powdered sugar

Small icing spatula

Silver star candies

they've set up completely, 10 to 15 minutes. Chilling the planets makes them easier to remove from the foil molds.

STEP 5: First, carefully pull back the foil from around the sides of the planet. Then gently pull the sides of the candy planet up and peel it off the foil. Remove all the planets and Saturn's rings from the foil molds. Place them on a plate that's been dusted with powdered sugar to prevent them from sticking.

All Together Now

Chop the gray coating chocolate pieces into small chunks. Attach Saturn's rings with a few dabs of buttercream. Spread a thin layer of buttercream over the backs of the planets to help them adhere to the cake. Using white buttercream will help the translucent gummy colors to pop against the dark galaxy finish. Add a cluster of gray coating chocolate chunks and star candies to form the asteroid belt.

CAKEQUATION

SUN BUTTER CAKE
(page 40)

+

RASPBERRY BUTTERCREAM
(page 61)

+

MILK CHOCOLATE-COATED CHOCOLATE CHIP COOKIE CLUSTERS
(page 88)

CHEWABLE PLANETS CAKE

Attain super space-queen status by not only making the main planets, but the dwarf planets as well.

Can't find white gummy bears? Trim the tummies off gummy frogs or sharks.

UNICORN thought

Candied Mandala Cake

Being a pastry chef can be a pretty lonely job. The hours and days you work are opposite those of the civilized working world. Even within the kitchen, the pastry chef is in before everyone else, and leaves just before or right as the rush of the evening service begins. When you work the line plating desserts at night, you're often in the back prepping while the line pumps out dinners. Then, you work your tail off slinging desserts while they scrub down and throw back a shift drink.

At one point, I remember feeling particularly sorry for myself while working in a very tough position for a demanding and slightly insane chef. In that moment of misery, I caught a story on the news about monks in Cambridge who had spent months creating a detailed mandala out of sand, only to bring their creation down to the Charles River and allow the wind to take it away. They were happy about it! Watching that beautiful image float away into thin air shocked me, but then made me happy, too. Spending my days creating intricate, time-consuming food under the eye of an unappreciative boss, just to watch my work disappear in one gulp, was driving me mad—but only because I was allowing it to. I set an intention to watch my work move through my hands with joy, and to not let the crazy lady get me down. Create your own edible mandala and watch it disappear into happy bellies.

The technique for creating all of these crispy fruit chips was a happy accident. One busy restaurant night, I was charged with making dried apple chip garnishes. What was supposed to be a quick dip in simple syrup ended up being an hours-long bath for my whisper-thin apple slices. I was certain the chips were ruined, but I dried out the slices anyway to see if they were salvageable. My recovery mission ended up being a revelation. The bright white chips dried perfectly flat and crispy—not a curled edge or brown spot in sight.

😎 **FAUX FABULOUS:** *For a less time-consuming, but equally Zen and chewier experience, create a mandala using various kinds of store-bought dried fruits and nuts.*

➡️

8-inch round layer cake, finished with a rustic vanilla buttercream finish (see page 104)

4 cups granulated sugar

4 cups water

1 medium saucepan

1 pineapple, peeled

Carrots, in assorted colors

1 apple

4 small heatproof storage containers

Vegetable peeler

Small knife

Chef's knife or mandolin slicer

Offset spatula

Small flower cookie cutter

Heavy-duty aluminum foil

Silicone baking mat or parchment paper

Soaking Syrup

In a medium saucepan, bring the sugar and water to a boil. Reduce the heat to medium-low and simmer for 5 to 7 minutes. Turn off the heat and leave the saucepan on the stove while you work on the fruit.

Crisp Candied Fruit Chips

STEP 1: Using a sharp knife or mandolin, cut paper-thin slices of the pineapple. Place the slices in a small heatproof container. Pour enough soaking syrup into the container so that all of the pineapple is submerged. Cover the container with foil and poke a few holes in the foil to release steam. Pop the container in the fridge to cool for at least 4 hours or up to overnight.

STEP 2: Peel the rough, outer skin off the carrots.

Cut the differently-colored carrots into 3- to 4-inch-long pieces. Trim one side of a piece so that it sits flat. Make another cut into the side of that carrot at an angle toward the first cut. The carrot stick should look like a long triangle with one rounded edge. Slice the stick into paper-thin pieces. Repeat with the rest of the carrot chunks. Separate the carrot petals by color and put them into different containers. They need to be separated because the bright colors could become muddled if they're all soaked together. Pour the warm soaking syrup into each container. Cover and cool as in step 1.

STEP 3: Slice the apple in half horizontally. (It will feel SO weird the first time you do this. Who cuts an apple that way?) Remove the seeds from both sides. Notice that when an apple is cut this way, the seed pockets create a little star or blossom shape. Pick up one of the apple halves and cut paper-thin slices, working from the cut-side down. Repeat with the other side of the apple. Cut out the center of each apple slice using the small flower cutter, lining up the seed pockets with the petals on the cutter. Store, soak, and chill, same as in step 1.

STEP 4: Position a rack in the center of the oven and preheat to 200°F.

Remove the containers from the fridge. Strain the syrups and lay the soaked fruit pieces out on cookie sheets lined with silicone baking mats or parchment paper. Bake for 40 minutes to 1 hour. It may take more or less time depending on the humidity. Check smaller pieces for doneness first.

Using an offset spatula, carefully remove a chip from the baking mat and place on a cool plate. Chips are done when they harden to a crisp within a few minutes of being removed from the oven. If the chip remains pliable, return it to the oven to dry out longer.

UNICORN thought

Don't even think about tossing those syrups! The soak has infused them with fantastic fruit and veggie flavor. Save them for making killer cocktails or for sweetening tea. Store syrups in the fridge for up to 2 weeks.

STEP 5: To shape a pineapple chip, pick it up with both hands and pinch it in the center with your fingertips, making a little puff. Repeat with the rest of the pineapple chips. Use the puffs individually or pile them up to create a fluffy pineapple flower.

All Together Now

Your mandala is 100 percent your own creation. I cannot offer specific instructions beyond this point. Go where inspiration leads you.

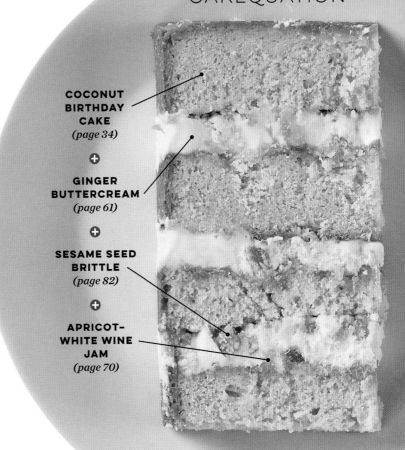

CAKEQUATION

COCONUT
BIRTHDAY
CAKE
(page 34)

✚

GINGER
BUTTERCREAM
(page 61)

✚

SESAME SEED
BRITTLE
(page 82)

✚

APRICOT–
WHITE WINE
JAM
(page 70)

- - - - - - - - - - - - - - - - - -

CANDIED MANDALA CAKE

Chapter 8

······························

COOKIE

DECORATING CAKES WITH COOKIES IS A TASTY WAY TO ADD rich textures and bold pops of color. By using sugar cookie dough, tuile batter, and meringue, it's easy to create cake decorations that have the same look and feel as those made with fondant, gum paste, or even buttercream. Super bonus: They taste good, too! Really good. Not, "Oh, I guess I don't mind that bite of chewy something-or-other along with my delicious layer cake" good, but "*good*" good. Don't get me wrong, fondant has its place. Cookies have their place, too—in my belly.

Sugar cookie dough shares many of fondant's sculptural qualities. It can be colored, rolled, molded, and even braided! Tuiles are super thin, delicate cookies that can be colored and shaped much like the way fine cake designers shape thin sheets of gum paste into flower petals. Many of the things you can do with buttercream can be done with meringue, too. Spread it, shape it, pipe it, and bake it into crispy cookies that add both dimension and flavor to your cake designs.

>> *Yields 2 cups cookie dough, enough to make 3 dozen 2- to 3-inch round cookies*

8 ounces unsalted butter, softened

1 cup granulated sugar

1 teaspoon baking powder

½ teaspoon kosher salt

1 teaspoon pure vanilla extract

1 large egg

3 cups all-purpose flour

Sugar Cookie Dough

➕ **DOCTOR, DOCTOR!** *Use store-bought cookie dough instead of making your own. Knead ½ cup of flour into one tube of sugar cookie dough to help prevent the dough from spreading.*

1. Position a rack in the center of the oven and preheat to 350°F. Line a cookie sheet with parchment paper.

2. In the bowl of a stand mixer fitted with the paddle attachment (or in a large bowl if using an electric hand mixer), beat the butter, sugar, baking powder, salt, and vanilla extract until light and fluffy, about 5 minutes, stopping occasionally to scrape down the sides of the bowl with a rubber spatula.

3. Add the egg and mix until combined, stopping to scrape down the sides of the bowl.

4. With the mixer on low, add the flour to the butter mixture until just incorporated. Prepare cookies based on your project's instructions or continue with steps 5 and 6. Color your sugar cookie dough at this point if your project calls for it.

5. To make rolled and cut sugar cookies: Lightly dust your work surface with flour. Roll the sugar cookie dough to ¾ inch thick, or whatever thickness your project calls for. Cut the dough into shapes using cookie cutters or a knife. Using a thin spatula, carefully move the cut shapes to the prepared cookie sheet, leaving an inch between cookies. Before baking, chill the dough in the fridge for at least 10 minutes or up to 3 days, covered.

UNICORN thought

To color sugar cookie dough, poke a hole in the dough and squirt in a few drops of gel coloring. Knead the color into the dough until the dough is uniform in color. Dust your work surface with flour if the dough gets sticky while kneading.

6. Bake for 7 to 9 minutes, until the cookies have lost their raw sheen and the edges are firm. Allow the cookies to cool on the cookie sheet for 5 minutes before moving to a plate or cooling rack.

7. Store cookies layered between parchment or wax paper in an airtight container for up to a week.

Make Ahead Tips

» Store batches of sugar cookie dough in the freezer, wrapped in plastic wrap and sealed in a zip-top bag, for up to 3 months.

» Roll sugar cookie dough between two pieces of parchment paper and store on a cookie sheet in the fridge until needed for up to a week. You can stack rolled sheets on top of one another on the same cookie sheet. Wrap the cookie sheet with plastic wrap and store in the freezer for up to 3 months. Pull individual sheets of dough from the freezer as needed.

» To freeze rolled and cut cookie shapes, place them on a cookie sheet in the freezer until frozen solid, about 30 minutes. Layer the shapes between pieces of parchment paper in an airtight container and freeze for up to 3 months. Pull cookie shapes right from the freezer and bake according to the recipe's instructions. Thin sugar cookie dough baked straight from the freezer doesn't require any additional baking time.

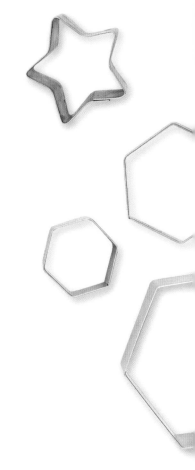

SUGAR COOKIE DOUGH VARIATIONS - - - - - - - - - - - - - - - - - -

Chocolate Sugar Cookie Dough	Reduce the flour by ½ cup. Add ½ cup Dutch-processed cocoa powder.
Black Velvet Sugar Cookie Dough	Reduce the flour by ½ cup. Add ¼ cup black cocoa powder and ¼ cup Dutch-processed cocoa powder.
Lemon Sugar Cookie Dough	Add 1 tablespoon grated lemon zest to the butter mixture before beating.
Almond Sugar Cookie Dough	Add 1 teaspoon almond extract to the butter mixture before beating.

» *Yields 1½ cups tuile batter, enough for about 2 dozen 2-inch round cookies*

6 large egg whites

1¾ cups granulated sugar

1¾ cups all-purpose flour

9 ounces unsalted butter, melted

Tuile Batter

1. Position a rack in the center of the oven and preheat to 350°F. Line cookie sheets with silicone baking mats or parchment paper.

2. Pour the egg whites into the bowl of a stand mixer (or into a large bowl if using an electric hand mixer) and whip on medium-high speed until frothy. Slowly pour in the sugar and continue to whip on medium-high speed until stiff peaks form, 5 to 7 minutes.

3. Fold the flour into the egg whites with a rubber spatula, ½ cup at a time. Fold in the melted butter until incorporated.

4. Use tuile batter right away or store in an airtight container in the fridge for 2 to 3 days. Press plastic wrap directly against the surface of the batter before putting the lid on the container to prevent it from forming a skin and absorbing fridge odors.

5. To make classic round tuiles: Spoon or pipe a teaspoon or so of batter for each tuile onto a lined cookie sheet. Bake for 5 to 7 minutes, until the edges of the tuiles have just started to brown. Shape baked tuiles as desired while they're still warm.

6. To make stenciled tuiles: Place a store-bought or homemade stencil (see Unicorn Thought) on the silicone mat. Pipe or spoon a small amount of batter into the middle of the stencil. Steady the stencil with one hand while using your other hand to spread the batter with an offset icing spatula. Return unused batter to the bowl. Carefully lift up the stencil, being mindful not to smudge the batter. Wipe off the stencil and repeat as needed. Baking times will vary depending on the size of your stenciled shape. The tuiles are done when the edges have just started to brown. Shape baked tuiles as desired while they're still warm.

7. To make piped tuiles: Fill a piping bag, paper cone, or squeeze bottle with tuile batter. Pipe words or shapes onto a lined cookie sheet. Piped shapes are typically very thin and will require very little baking time, 3 to 5 minutes, until the edges have just started to brown. Shape baked tuiles as desired while they're still warm.

Shaping Tips

» Have a plan before the tray goes into the oven. Tuiles firm up very quickly as they cool. Set up whatever you'll be using to shape your cookies (rolling pin, egg crate, etc.) before they go into the oven.

» Use an offset icing spatula (or other thin spatula) to quickly remove the tuiles from the cookie sheet. Slide the spatula under every part of the cookie to release it from the sheet and prevent the cookie from tearing.

» Since tuiles firm up quickly, make life easier and don't crowd the cookie sheet. Bake just a few at time until you get the hang of shaping the warm cookies.

» If you're comfortable doing so, leave the tray of tuiles in the oven with the door open and carefully pull them from the tray one by one. Work quickly to prevent the tuiles from overbaking.

» Re-soften tuiles that have set up by placing them back on the lined cookie sheet and into the oven for just a minute. You can typically get away with doing this once per cookie. By the second try, the cookie will likely be too hard to re-soften.

Hands down, the best material for making a tuile stencil is a fish tub lid. Yes, the lids from plastic storage containers that fish mongers use to deliver fresh fish to restaurants and markets. This is one of those universally-known secret facts among pastry chefs: Steal the flat, clean fish tub lids and hide them as fast as you can. I don't know what it is about this specific plastic lid, but it works perfectly. Fish tubs can be purchased directly from fish markets or from some restaurant supply stores. You might even try asking nicely for one at a fine dining establishment near you. Can't find a fish tub? Try any other flat, heavy plastic lid (deli container lids work in a pinch) or heavy cardstock that's been laminated. Make a stencil by drawing a shape onto the plastic and carefully cutting it out with a sharp craft knife.

UNICORN thought

6-inch round layer cake, finished with salted caramel buttercream (page 60)

Tuile Batter (page 144)

Burgundy, orange, and yellow gel food coloring

Fish tub lid (see Unicorn Thought, page 145) or clear take-out food container lid (or any kind of flat, heavy plastic)

Black permanent marker

Scissors or craft knife

Leaf templates (page 227), optional

Small offset spatula

Silicone baking mat

Empty egg carton

Heavy-duty aluminum foil

Autumn Crisps Cake

If you've ever wanted to make tuile cookies, this is the perfect cake design to start with. Tuiles are delicate and finicky, so they can take a few tries to master. You may have a cookie tear as you try to lift it from the baking mat. Or, one might not set up quite as you wanted it to. The beauty of this design is, it doesn't matter! Autumn leaves are naturally a beautiful, crumpled mess. My kind of design!

Make the leaves in shades of green for a spring or summer celebration, or leave the tuile batter un-colored for a more subtle, monochromatic look.

Position a rack in the center of the oven and preheat to 350°F. Line a cookie sheet with a silicone baking mat.

STEP 1: Divide the batter equally among three small bowls. Use the gel food coloring to tint the batters burgundy, orange, and yellow.

STEP 2: Place the plastic lid on top of the leaf templates and trace them using a black permanent marker, or draw the leaves freehand. Carefully cut out the stencils using scissors or a craft knife, then discard the leaf shape, leaving the stencil. Cut the lid to separate the three stencils.

STEP 3: Place one of the stencils on the silicone baking mat and use a small offset spatula to fill the stencil with a thin layer of one of the colored tuile batters. Lift the stencil up and move to a clear space on the baking mat to spread another cookie. Wipe the stencil clean as needed. Fill the mat with no more than 6 cookies at a time. Tuiles set up very quickly, so it's best to work in small batches.

→

UNICORN thought

Use the remaining tuile batter to create a giant leaf cookie. Place the cookie on a platter and use it to serve small bites like truffles or cut fruit. Your guests will think you're unbe-leaf-able.

To create an ombré effect, spread one color of batter over half of the stencil and another colored batter over the other half. Swipe the offset spatula over the entire stencil to blend the colors together.

STEP 4: Bake the tuiles for 7 to 10 minutes, until the edges of the cookies just start to turn the lightest shade of brown. Because tuiles are so thin, they can overbake in only a minute or two. Keep a close eye on your first batch to see how quickly they finish in your oven. Bake only one sheet of tuiles at a time.

While the tuiles are baking, use a large sheet of aluminum foil to line the inside of an egg carton. Press the foil into the cups, creating peaks and valleys. Keep the lined egg carton nearby.

STEP 5: Remove the tray of tuiles from the oven. Use the offset spatula to lift one of the leaves off the baking mat. Drape the leaf over the foil, letting it crumple and droop like a real leaf. Quickly repeat this step, one by one, until all the tuiles have been removed from the baking sheet. If some should harden before you get to them, pop the sheet back into the oven for just a few seconds to re-soften the tuiles. If the tuiles don't re-soften, just use them flat (or eat them).

Repeat this process until you have at least two dozen leaves.

All Together Now

Tuiles will begin to soften the longer they sit against the buttercream, so assemble the cake shortly before serving. Cover the sides of the cake with leaf tuiles, pile a few on top of the cake, or save a few leaves to garnish slices when serving.

CAKEQUATION

SWEET POTATO CAKE
(page 45)

+

CREAM CHEESE FROSTING
(page 66)

+

CANDIED PECAN CRUNCH
(page 80)

AUTUMN CRISPS CAKE

Floral Crown Cake

I started pastry chef-ing shortly before garnishing plated desserts with elaborate tuiles went out of style (at least in New England). In that time, I made tuiles in the shapes of bananas, treble clefs, swirls, corkscrews, and just about every sleek, geometric shape imaginable. I was a good line-mate and would do my best to bulk up the station's tuile supply for the next person. At one restaurant, a cook (who typically worked the garde manger or salad station) would plate desserts on my days off. I used to dread my first day back on. I knew I was in for a harried night of tuile-making catch-up. He didn't earn the nickname Mashy Meatball Hands for nothing.

Don't worry if you also feel like Mashy Meatball Hands when you first start working with tuiles. Their thin, delicate nature is what makes them so wonderful, but also so frustrating. Stick with it and you'll be rewarded with stunning cake decor that will leave your guests wondering how you did it. Consider a broken tuile as a little bonus snack. Or in Mashy's case, dessert for a week.

😎 **FAUX FABULOUS:** *Make simple flowers using round store-bought wafer cookies as the petals, and send someone out to the Italian bakery to pick up a box of leaf cookies.*

//

Position a rack in the center of the oven and preheat to 350°F. Line a cookie sheet with a silicone baking mat.

STEP 1: Divide the tuile batter among three small bowls. Dye one bowl of batter pale pink and another gray. Leave the third bowl uncolored.

STEP 2: Place the plastic lid on top of the two petal templates and trace them using a black permanent marker, or draw them freehand. Carefully cut along the lines using scissors or a craft knife, then discard the shape, leaving the stencil. Cut the lid to separate the two stencils, making them easier to work with.

➡️

8-inch round layer cake, finished with pale pink buttercream and piped ruffles (see page 104)

1 batch Tuile Batter (page 144)

Pink, white, and black gel food coloring

1 cup black coating chocolate or tinted dark chocolate

Fish tub lid (see Unicorn Thought, page 145) or clear take-out food container lid (or any kind of flat, heavy plastic)

Piping bags or paper cones

Small offset spatula

Black permanent marker

Scissors or craft knife

Petal templates (page 226), optional

Silicone baking mat

Small bowls

Dish towel

Heavy-duty aluminum foil

See the same blooms in brighter colors on page 242.

STEP 3: Place the large petal stencil on the silicone baking mat. Spread pink batter inside the rounded edge of the petal. Use a small offset spatula to fill the rest of the stencil with a thin layer of white batter. Swipe the spatula over the entire stencil to blend the colors together. Lift up the stencil and move it to a clear space on the baking mat. Repeat this process four times, making at least five large petals total. Wipe the stencil clean as needed. Repeat the same process with the small petal stencil and make the same quantity for each flower.

STEP 4: Bake the tuiles for 7 to 10 minutes, until the edges of the cookies just start to turn the lightest shade of brown. Because tuiles are so thin, they can overbake in only a minute or two. Keep a close eye on your first batch to see how quickly they finish in your oven. Bake only one sheet of tuiles at a time.

STEP 5: Remove the tray of tuiles from the oven. Use the offset spatula to lift one of the petals off the baking mat. Place the petal into a small bowl to set up. Quickly repeat this step, one by one, until all of the tuiles have been removed from the baking mat. If some should harden before you get to them, pop the sheet back into the oven for a few seconds to re-soften the tuiles. If the tuiles don't re-soften, just use them flat toward the back of the finished flower.

➡️

Like what you see here? Chocolate flowers are made in a very similar way. Turn your cake into a mixed media masterpiece by adding a few chocolate blooms or leaves (pages 199, 205, 208, and 213).

Lose a petal from one of your finished blooms? Be sneaky, like me, and tuck the broken side close to another flower. It'll make the cluster look more realistic and like you meant to do it.

STEP 6: Line a small bowl with heavy-duty aluminum foil.

Melt the black coating chocolate and pour it into a piping bag or cone. Snip the tip and pipe a quarter-sized puddle of chocolate into the lined bowl. Place the pointed end of a large petal into the puddle. Repeat with more petals, positioning the petals to overlap the edges as you go. Set the flower aside until the chocolate hardens, about 10 minutes. Pipe a small mound of chocolate into the center of the flower to finish it. Allow the chocolate to harden completely before using the flower on the cake, about 10 minutes.

STEP 7: Repeat steps 3 through 6 to make more flowers in each size.

STEP 8: Fill a piping bag with the gray tuile batter. Snip the tip and pipe squiggly-edged leaf shapes to mimic dusty miller leaves (a popular silvery-gray filler foliage). Bake as you did with the petals. To give the leaves subtle movement, drape them over a clean, scrunched-up dish towel to set up.

All Together Now

Tuiles will begin to soften the longer they sit against the buttercream, so assemble the cake shortly before serving.

Start the arrangement by placing the largest flower close to the edge of the cake. Place smaller blossoms around the centerpiece flower. Tuck dusty miller leaves around the flowers.

CAKEQUATION

ZUCCHINI CAKE
(page 45)

+

LIME CURD
(page 65)

+

CANDIED ALMOND CRUNCH
(page 80)

+

YOUR FAVORITE VANILLA BUTTERCREAM
(page 55)

FLORAL CROWN CAKE

6-inch round layer cake, finished with chocolate buttercream (page 60)

Tuile Batter (page 144)

Sugar Cookie Dough (page 142)

Red, blue, yellow, dark green, and light green gel food coloring

Chocolate candies, various sizes

Rolling pin

Dinosaur cookie cutters

Fish tub lid or clear take-out food container lid (or any kind of flat, heavy plastic; see Unicorn Thought on page 145)

Black permanent marker

Scissors or a craft knife

Leaf templates (pages 226–227), optional

Piping bag or paper cone

Small offset spatula

Parchment paper

Dish towel

Silicone baking mat

Can You Dig It? Cake

Big scary animals are not my favorite thing in the world. I'm not a fan of claws, pinchers, or mouths full of sharp teeth. When charged with making a cake of an animal that I'm not a fan of (shark, dinosaur, miniature pony, lobster, etc.), I employ one of two strategies: (1) Make the creature as adorable as possible with giant kawaii eyes; or (2) Add as few identifying details as possible and pretend I'm doing so as a design statement. Who wants to stare at some dead-eyed lizard for an hour while piping its facial details onto a cookie. Not me!

These brightly colored cookies offer a nice contrast to the chocolate-brown dirt details and natural-colored leaves. Customize the design by creating dinos in the birthday boy or girl's favorite colors.

///

Position a rack in the center of the oven and preheat to 350°F. Line one cookie sheet with parchment paper and another with a silicone baking mat.

Dinosaurs

STEP 1: Divide the sugar cookie dough into three equal parts. Use the gel food coloring to dye one part red, one yellow, and the other blue.

STEP 2: Roll the dough, one color at a time, to about ⅛ inch thick. Lightly dust your work surface with flour as needed to prevent the dough from sticking. Cut out dinosaur shapes and place them on the parchment-lined cookie sheet. Pop the sheet in the fridge until the cookies are completely chilled, at least 20 minutes.

STEP 3: Bake the cookies for 7 to 9 minutes, until they've lost their raw sheen and the edges have just started to brown. Place the cookie sheets on a rack to cool, about 15 minutes. Don't move the cookies until they've cooled to the touch, as warm, thin cookies might crack. Once

UNICORN thought

As you fill the cake, sprinkle each layer of filling with bone-shaped sprinkles or candies. Partygoers will feel like they're on a tasty archeological dig.

the cookies are cool enough to handle, use a spatula to move them to a flat plate or room-temperature cookie sheet to continue cooling. The cookies need to lose any hint of warmth before you place them on the cake—otherwise, they will melt the buttercream.

Leaves

STEP 1: Use a few drops of yellow gel food coloring to dye about 2 tablespoons of the tuile batter. Divide the rest of the batter into two bowls. Dye one half light green and the other dark green.

STEP 2: Place the plastic lid on top of the leaf templates and trace them using a black permanent marker, or draw them freehand. I used the large rounded leaf and maple leaf templates, but you can use whatever leaf shapes you want. Carefully cut along the lines using scissors or a craft knife, then discard the leaf shape, leaving the stencil. Cut the lid to separate the stencils, making them easier to work with.

STEP 3: Place the rounded leaf stencil on the silicone baking mat and use a small offset spatula to fill the stencil with a thin layer of light green tuile batter. Lift up the stencil and move to a clear space on the baking mat to spread another cookie. Wipe the stencil clean as needed. Repeat at least four times, making as many cookies as you'd like.

Repeat the same process with the other leaf stencil and the dark green tuile batter. Make at least four leaves.

STEP 4: Pour the yellow tuile batter into a piping bag or paper cone. Snip the tip off the bag and pipe thin detail lines on the large rounded leaves. Draw a center line and thin vein lines.

STEP 5: Bake the tuiles for 7 to 10 minutes, until the edges of the cookies just start to turn the lightest shade of brown. Because tuiles are so thin, they can overbake in only a minute or two. Keep a close eye on your first batch to see how quickly they finish in your oven. Bake only one sheet of tuiles at a time.

While the tuiles are baking, place a rolling pin, small bowl, spatula, etc., onto a dish towel to keep steady. Remove the tuiles from the oven. Slide a small offset spatula under one of the tuiles to release it from the baking mat. Quickly and carefully drape the tuile over one of the items on the dish towel, the way a real leaf would naturally fall. Repeat this step, one by one, until all the tuiles have been removed from the baking mat. If some should harden before you get to them, pop the sheet back into the oven for just a few seconds to re-soften the tuiles. If the tuiles don't re-soften, just use them flat.

Make extra leaves and use them to garnish cake slices. Inform people as they eat them that cookie leaves were the preferred food of partysaurus rex.

UNICORN thought

All Together Now

Tuiles will soften the longer they sit against the buttercream, so assemble the cake shortly before serving.

Press chocolate candies onto the sides of the cake to resemble layers of sediment. Make horizontal rows of similar candies all around the sides of the cake.

Arrange the tuile leaves on the top and around the sides of the cake in tropical-looking clusters. Tuck the dinosaur cookies in and around the groups of leaves. Serve any extra cookies on platters or use them to garnish cake slices.

CAKEQUATION

CHOCOLATE BIRTHDAY CAKE
(page 37)

+

MARSHMALLOW
(page 76)

+

CANDY-COATED GRAHAM CRACKER CLUSTERS
(page 90)

+

CHOCOLATE BUTTERCREAM
(page 60)

CAN YOU DIG IT? CAKE

Pretty Kitty Cake

Every animal my two-year-old daughter, Violet, sees is a kitty. Squirrel, kitty. Dog, kitty. Goats at the petting zoo, yep, kitties. She also loves cookies. Combine the two and voilà! The cake of her cat-obsessed, cookie-monster dreams.

Using a sugar cookie as a cake topper is an underused technique in cake design, IMHO. I know I'm not alone when I tell you that I have dozens and dozens of cookie cutters that I will never, ever, ever use to make pristinely piped sugar cookie masterpieces. Get more use out of your cookie cutters (or actually use them) by thinking of the dough as the decorative element *instead* of the icing. Add a few simple details and you'll have your guests convinced that you're a minimalist cookie design genius. See a rainbow variation of the teeny heart cookies on page x.

😎 **FAUX FABULOUS:** *No time for a custom topper? Stick a store-bought sugar cookie onto a lollipop for instant cake coolness.*

Skip the cut and repeat and create a Swiss dot pattern on the sides of the cake using candy hearts, chocolate chips, or mini M&M's flipped upside-down.

//

STEP 1: Roll the black velvet sugar cookie dough to about ⅛ inch thick. Lightly flour the surface as needed to keep the dough from sticking, or roll the dough between two pieces of parchment paper.

STEP 2: Cut 1 large cat face, 10 small cat faces, and 60 hearts from the dough. Gather and reroll the dough as needed. Use an offset spatula to carefully move the cut shapes to parchment-lined cookie sheets.

Cut two rounds from the remaining dough. Move the rounds to one of the parchment-lined cookie sheets. Place the round cutter back over one of the circles of dough so that one edge of the cutter cuts through the circle about midway. Remove the top portion of dough, leaving an almond shape behind, creating one of the cat's eyes. Repeat with the other circle. Pop the cookie sheets into the fridge until the dough is chilled completely, at least 20 minutes.

→

6-inch round layer cake, finished in mint green buttercream

Black Velvet Sugar Cookie Dough (page 143)

Gold luster dust

Clear extract or grain alcohol

Pink heart-shaped sprinkle

1 cup black coating chocolate or colored dark chocolate

Lollipop stick

Rolling pin

Parchment paper

Small offset spatula

Large cat face cookie cutter (4 inches wide)

Small cat face cookie cutter (¾ inch wide)

Heart cookie cutter (¾ inch wide)

Round cookie cutter (1½ inches)

Fine-tipped paintbrush

Small bowl

Ruler or straight-edge

STEP 3: Position a rack in the center of the oven and preheat to 350°F.

Bake the cookies for 5 to 7 minutes, until they've lost their raw sheen and the edges are firm. Place the cookie sheets on a rack to cool, about 15 minutes. Don't move the cookies until they've cooled to the touch, as warm, thin cookies might crack. Once the cookies are cool enough to handle, use a spatula to move them to a flat plate or room-temperature cookie sheet to continue cooling. The cookies need to lose any hint of warmth before you place them on the cake—otherwise, they will melt the buttercream.

STEP 4: Use the offset spatula to carefully remove the large cat face and two almond-shaped cookies from the cookie sheet. Flip the cat face over. Melt the black coating chocolate and dip the end of the lollipop stick into the melted chocolate. Place the stick on the back of the cookie, letting the un-dipped portion of the stick hang over the bottom edge of the cookie. Allow the chocolate to harden, about 5 minutes.

Flip the cookie back over. Using a few dabs of melted chocolate, attach the almond-shaped cookies to the front of the cat face. Dip the back of the heart sprinkle into the melted chocolate and place it onto the cookie as the cat's nose. Allow the chocolate to harden, about 5 minutes.

UNICORN thought

Whip up a few extra kitties and sneak them into lunch boxes throughout the week. When the kids ask where they came from, shrug and point to the cat.

STEP 5: In a small bowl, combine approximately 1 teaspoon gold luster dust with a few drops of clear extract or grain alcohol. Add just enough liquid for the mixture to form a paste. Using a fine-tipped paintbrush, paint the cat's eyes gold, leaving a long, thin, almond-shaped area empty in the center of each eye.

All Together Now

Arrange the tiny hearts on the sides of the cake in a Swiss dot pattern: Start the first row by placing a heart on the buttercream just above the bottom of the cake. Place the next heart below the top edge of the cake, directly above the first heart. Add a third heart between the first two hearts. Place another heart between the top and middle ones. Add the last heart between the bottom and middle ones. Add a small cat face instead of a heart every few dots or so. You can use a ruler or straight-edge if you need a guide, but I always prefer to eyeball my Swiss dot patterns. Push the lollipop stick into the center of the top of the cake.

CAKEQUATION

BLACK VELVET BIRTHDAY CAKE
(page 38)

+

STRAWBERRY BUTTERCREAM
(page 61)

+

DARK CHOCOLATE GANACHE
(page 62)

+

DARK CHOCOLATE-COATED CHOCOLATE COOKIE CLUSTERS
(page 88)

PRETTY KITTY CAKE

6-inch round layer cake stacked on top of an 8-inch round cake, finished with sprinkle-speckled buttercream (see page 104)

Sugar Cookie Dough (page 142)

Red, yellow, blue, and black gel food coloring

Whole peanuts in the shell

Animal cookie cutters: monkey, elephant, seal, giraffe, gorilla, zebra, tiger

Round cookie cutter (1½ inches)

Rolling pin

Parchment paper

Small offset spatula

Small sharp knife

Three-Ring Circus Cake

This cake was inspired by Japanese cookie artists who use layers of colored doughs, instead of colored icings, to create adorable critters and tasty landscapes. I was first introduced to this kind of cookie-making by an image I saw online of a tiny teddy bear cookie hugging an almond. I immediately jumped down the interweb-rabbit hole and found dozens of inspiring images, books, and blogs dedicated to this style of cookie crafting.

I find these cookies so appealing because I am not a happy piper. Intricately detailed cookie designs are a thing of beauty, but piping is a skill that requires much practice and patience to master. Not to mention, many small tools to keep track of and clean. I have the utmost respect for cookie decorators who have laser focus and a steady hand, but I am not one of them. Making cookies by rolling, squishing, and cutting (with little cleanup)—that's my jam.

😎 **FAUX FABULOUS:** *Simplify your circus by using animal crackers instead of custom-colored cookies. Cut up peanut butter cups and flip them upside-down to use as pedestals. Give the critters candy balls or round sprinkle quins to play with.*

//

Plain Animals and Balls

STEP 1: Roll the cookie dough into a large log. Divide the dough into six equal parts. Divide one of the dough parts in half: Use gel food coloring to tint one of the small parts red and the other blue. Set one part of plain dough aside. Color the remaining parts black, gray, orange, and yellow.

STEP 2: Roll and cut each dough portion individually. Roll the dough about ⅛ inch thick. Lightly dust your work surface with flour as needed to prevent the dough from sticking. Cut at least 1 animal and a total of 12 rounds from the colored doughs:

» **ORANGE:** monkey

» **GRAY:** elephant and seal

» **YELLOW:** giraffe and rounds

» **BLUE:** rounds

» **RED:** rounds

» **BLACK:** gorilla

STEP 3: Use an offset spatula to move the cut animals and rounds to a parchment-lined cookie sheet. Wrap the elephant's trunk around a peanut. Place another peanut into one of the monkey's arms and wrap the hand up around the peanut to hold it in place. Pinch off pea-sized pieces of orange dough. Roll them into tiny balls between your fingertips. Flatten the balls and press them onto the giraffe's back and neck to create a simple pattern.

Pedestals

STEP 1: Gather small pieces of the plain and black doughs, each about the size of a golf ball. Roll each dough ball into a log. Line up the logs next to each other to create stripes. Use a rolling pin to carefully roll the striped dough flat. Roll in the direction of the stripes to prevent the pattern from warping.

STEP 2: Use a small, sharp knife to cut the striped dough into rectangles. Cut off the short ends of the rectangle at an angle to create the pedestal shape. Make at least three pedestals. Use an offset spatula to move the cut shapes to a parchment-lined cookie sheet.

Marbled Animals

STEP 1: Pinch off pieces of the plain and black cookie doughs, each about the size of a golf ball. Roll the balls into long, thin ropes. Twist the ropes together, then bend the twisted rope back over itself. Squish the loop of twisted dough flat. Repeat the rolling, twisting, bending, and squishing process to achieve thinner, swirled stripes.

UNICORN thought

Not wild about the circus? Use the same techniques to create a cake decorated with a clowder of frisky kitties or pack of perky puppies.

STEP 2: Roll the marbled dough to about ⅛ inch thick. Dust your work surface with flour as needed. Place a zebra cookie cutter on the dough so that the marbled stripes run vertically throughout the shape. Cut out the shape. Use an offset spatula to move the cut shape to a parchment-lined cookie sheet.

STEP 3: Repeat the same marbling, rolling, and cutting process with the orange and black doughs for the tiger. Use an offset spatula to move the cut shape to a parchment-lined cookie sheet.

STEP 4: Pop the cookie sheets into the fridge until the dough shapes are chilled completely, at least 20 minutes.

STEP 5: Position a rack in the center of the oven and preheat to 350°F.

Bake the cookies for 7 to 9 minutes, until they've lost their raw sheen and the edges are set. Place the cookie sheets on a rack to cool, about 15 minutes. Don't move the cookies until they've cooled to the touch, as warm, thin cookies might crack. Once the cookies are cool enough to handle, use a spatula to move them to a flat plate or room-temperature cookie sheet to continue cooling before placing them on the cake.

All Together Now

Arrange the pedestal, animal, and ball cookies on the sides and top of the cake to create a playful circus scene.

CAKEQUATION

PEANUT
BUTTER
CAKE
(page 40)

✚

PEANUT
BRITTLE
(page 82)

✚

BUTTERED
POPCORN
GANACHE
(page 64)

✚

YOUR FAVORITE
VANILLA
BUTTERCREAM
(page 55)

THREE-RING CIRCUS CAKE

Sweater Weather Cake

Leggings and sweater weather: the most wonderful time of the year! This cake just screams cozy, both inside and out. As is, it's an amazing fall dessert. Change up the colors to shades of blue, and it's totally nautical. Create twists in soft pastels for a cuddly, textured baby shower cake. Go totally white-on-white for a stunning and simple winter holiday cake.

😎 **FAUX FABULOUS:** *Keep the mixer unplugged and use store-bought dough. Buy a no-spread dough or knead ½ to 1 cup of flour into a tube of sugar cookie dough to keep it from spreading.*

///

STEP 1: Divide the sugar cookie dough in half. Set one half aside and divide the remaining half into four equal parts. Divide the chocolate cookie dough into four equal parts. Set aside one piece of the chocolate dough. Knead one of the remaining pieces of chocolate dough and two pieces of the plain dough together. Set that aside. Knead the remaining pieces of dough together. When completed, you should have four different amounts of dough, each in a different shade. Roll each piece of dough into a log. Roll all the logs to the same length (the diameters will all be different).

STEP 2: Line up the logs in no particular order. Squeeze and roll them all together to form one large log. Twist the log and bend it in half back over itself. Squeeze it back into a log and repeat the twisting, bending, and rolling process. Cover the marbled log of dough with plastic wrap and place it in the fridge to rest for at least an hour, or up to overnight.

STEP 3: Remove the plastic wrap and divide the log into eight equal parts. Working in sections for these next steps will help the cookie pieces maintain their beautiful marbled look without muddling the colors.

STEP 4: Roll one piece of dough into a pencil-thin rope. Bend the rope in half, bringing the ends together. Twist both sides of the rope together. Measure the height of your cake, then cut the rope into lengths of the same size. Move the pieces to a parchment-lined cookie sheet. Repeat with the remaining dough.

→

6-inch round layer cake, finished with chocolate buttercream (page 60)

2 batches Sugar Cookie Dough (page 142)

1 batch Chocolate Sugar Cookie Dough (page 143)

Ruler

Knife

Dazzle those around you with your advanced planning skills. Make and freeze the unbaked cookies ahead of time. Bake the cookies straight from the freezer shortly before you need them.

UNICORN thought

STEP 5: Pop the shaped dough pieces into the fridge until they have chilled completely, at least 30 minutes or up to overnight.

STEP 6: Position a rack in the center of the oven and preheat to 350°F.

Bake the cookies for 8 to 10 minutes, until they've lost their raw sheen and are firm to the touch. Set the cookie sheets on a rack to cool for about 15 minutes. Don't move the cookies until they've cooled to the touch—you don't want to warp the beautiful shape you worked so hard to achieve. Once the cookies are cool enough to handle, use a spatula to move them to a flat plate or room-temperature cookie sheet to continue cooling. The cookies need to lose any hint of warmth before you place them on the cake— otherwise, they will melt the buttercream.

All Together Now

Press the cookies onto the sides of the cake, lining up one after the other all the way around. Extra cookies can be served on the side or stored at room temperature in an airtight container for up to 5 days.

CAKEQUATION

MOCHA
BIRTHDAY
CAKE
(page 38)

ESPRESSO
BUTTERCREAM
(page 61)

ALMOND NUT
BUTTER
CRUNCH
(page 85)

SWEATER WEATHER CAKE

Bird Food Cake

One of the most important things any chef or pastry chef learns is not to put any garnish or element on the plate that doesn't enhance the dish. And under NO circumstances do you put something on the plate that isn't edible! Those rules, which were so ingrained in my way of thinking during my early pastry-chef days, eventually drew me out of the high-end cake design world to where I am today. There is certainly a time and a place for exquisitely sculpted, intricate (but marginally edible) cake decorations. Creating impressive centerpiece cakes for weddings and large-scale events is a true art unto itself. But for this pastry chef-turned-cake maker-turned-whatever it is that I am right now, I knew there had to be a better way—that truly edible and delicious cake decorations could be made to elevate both the overall flavor profile and the appearance of a cake. This cake design was one of the first to come from that exploratory process. Here, the classic sliced almond flower is upgraded, blown up, and given an extreme wine-dipped makeover, turning the ordinary into something extraordinary.

My directions for this cake are purposefully vague. It would be impossible for me to tell you how many sliced almonds or pecans you should use for any particular flower, because every nut is different. Use these instructions as a general guideline for creating your own beautifully delicious flower cookies with what's available to you.

//

Branches

STEP 1: Place the 8-inch cake pan on a piece of parchment paper and trace the outline of the pan with the black permanent marker. Flip over the paper and place on a cookie sheet.

STEP 2: Pinch off a piece of chocolate sugar cookie dough about the size of a large grape. Roll the dough into an imperfect, pencil-thin log. Cut the log into pieces and arrange them within the circle, just as you'd like the branches to appear on top of the finished cake. Tuck some pistachios into the dough to mimic buds on branches. Pop the cookie sheet into the fridge until the dough has chilled thoroughly, at least 20 minutes.

→

8-inch round layer cake, finished in honey buttercream (page 60)

Sugar Cookie Dough (page 142)

Chocolate Sugar Cookie Dough (page 143)

Sliced almonds

Slivered almonds

Pecan halves

Pistachios

Hazelnuts

Poppy seeds

Sesame seeds

Red wine (or gel food coloring and water)

Cooking spray

Round cookie cutters

Small knife

8-inch round cake pan

Rolling pin

Parchment paper

Black permanent marker

Standard muffin tin

Mini muffin tin

STEP 3: Position a rack in the center of the oven and preheat to 350°F.

Bake the logs for 7 to 9 minutes, until they've lost their raw sheen and are firm to the touch. Place the cookie sheet on a rack until cool, at least 20 minutes. The branches are thin and delicate, so allow them to cool completely before moving them to the cake to avoid breakage.

Open Flowers

STEP 1: Pinch off a piece of sugar cookie dough (either one) about the size of a grape and roll it into a ball. Dip your fingertips in cold water and roll the ball between your fingers to lightly dampen the surface. Roll the ball in chopped nuts or seeds.

STEP 2: Place the coated ball into the well of a greased standard muffin tin. Stick nuts all the way around the sides of the ball to create the flower's petals. Prop up the outer edges of the nuts along the sides of the muffin tin. Repeat with any combination of dough, nuts, and seeds that you'd like. Pop the muffin tin into the fridge until the dough has chilled thoroughly, at least 20 minutes.

STEP 3: Bake the balls for 8 to 10 minutes, until they're firm to the touch. Place the muffin tin on a rack and allow the cookies to cool for at least 20 minutes before removing them from the tin.

STEP 4: Make smaller flowers using the same processes in steps 1 and 2, except with smaller balls of dough (about the size of a pea) and smaller nuts. Bake the flowers in the mini muffin tin, following the baking instructions in step 3.

Ruffled Flowers

STEP 1: Tint sliced almonds by soaking them overnight in red wine or water tinted with food coloring.

Strain the wine and dump the colored nuts onto cookie sheets lined with paper towels. Dry off the nuts before using.

STEP 2: Pinch off a piece of sugar cookie dough (either one) about the size of a grape and roll it into a ball. Place the ball on a parchment-lined cookie sheet. Cup your hand over the ball of dough, flattening the bottom against the parchment paper. The cookie should look like a little dome.

→

No one likes a bad nut. Keep your nuts fresher longer by keeping them cold. Store nuts in the fridge for up to 6 months or in the freezer for up to 1 year. Use them straight out of the fridge or freezer in any recipe.

UNICORN thought

STEP 3: Stick pieces of nuts into the dough, starting around the outer edge and working your way toward the center of the cookie. Make the cookie as full as you'd like, adding more nuts as needed. Pop the sheet into the fridge until the cookie has chilled thoroughly, at least 20 minutes. I made one large ruffled cookie for the cake pictured, but you can make as many as you'd like. Get creative and use either dough, change up the sizes of the balls, and try different varieties of nuts.

STEP 4: Bake the cookie for 8 to 10 minutes, until it's firm. Place the cookie sheet on a rack to cool for at least 20 minutes. Allow the cookie to cool completely before placing on the cake.

Folded Flowers

STEP 1: Roll sugar cookie dough (either one) to about ⅛ inch thick. Lightly dust your work surface with flour as needed to prevent the dough from sticking.

STEP 2: Cut out rounds in various sizes. Use a small knife to make six evenly spaced cuts around the outer edge of a round. Make cuts that are about one-third of the round's diameter deep.

STEP 3: Pinch off a piece of sugar cookie dough (either one) large enough that, when rolled into a ball, it fits in the center of a dough round without overlapping any of the cuts. Dip your fingertips in water and roll the ball to lightly dampen the surface. Roll the ball in chopped nuts or seeds, and place it in the center of the dough round.

STEP 4: Lift up one of the dough tabs and press it against the center of the ball, gently pulling on the edges to wrap the tab around the side of the ball. Repeat with the rest of the tabs, overlapping as you go. Repeat with rounds in various combinations and sizes. Pop the sheet into the fridge until the cookies have chilled thoroughly, at least 20 minutes.

STEP 5: Bake the cookies for 10 to 12 minutes, until they've lost their raw sheen and are firm to the touch. Place the cookie sheet on a rack to cool for at least 20 minutes. Allow the cookies to cool completely before placing them onto the cake.

Acorns

STEP 1: Roll chocolate sugar cookie dough to about ⅛ inch thick. Lightly dust your work surface with flour as needed to prevent the dough from sticking.

STEP 2: Use a tiny round cutter or the end of a round piping tip to cut a dough round small enough to fit over the thick end of a hazelnut. Dip the tip of your finger in water and run it over the surface of the dough. Stick the damp side of the dough to the fat end of a hazelnut. Insert a sliver of pecan or almond into the center of the acorn cap to create the stem. Repeat with more hazelnuts. Place them on a parchment-lined cookie sheet and pop into the fridge until the cookie caps have chilled thoroughly, at least 10 minutes.

STEP 3: Bake the acorns for 7 to 9 minutes, until the dough is firm to the touch. Place the cookie sheet on a rack to cool for at least 20 minutes before handling. Allow the nuts to cool completely before placing them onto the cake.

All Together Now

Use an offset spatula to carefully move the chocolate cookie branches onto the top of the cake. Arrange the completed nut flowers in a crescent-shape design along the edge of the cake. Add the largest flowers first, then fill in with the smaller flowers before completing the design with the acorns.

CAKEQUATION

CARROT
CAKE
(page 45)

+

BROWN
BUTTER
CREAM
CHEESE
FROSTING
(page 67)

+

SUNFLOWER
SEED
BRITTLE
(page 82)

BIRD FOOD CAKE

Showers of Love Cake

Whether you're showering a mom-to-be with love and onesies or a future bride with glassware and good wishes, this cake will fit the bill. Customize the design with the future baby's monogram or the couple's shared initial. Match the party's decor by changing up the color of the raindrops, monogram, sky, or even tinting the clouds. Add a moon or sun on a stick, and you've got a sweet celestial birthday cake.

Those variations on this cake are great examples of the times we get together to share a meal and delight in a loved one's good fortune. But I don't always eat cake when I'm happy. Sometimes I eat cake when I'm sad. Sometimes I want a piece of cake because something really crappy happened, and a slice (or two, don't judge) of chocolate cake is just what the doctor ordered. Maybe a good friend is going through a breakup, lost a job, or is getting audited by the IRS. We have cards to send during such times, but very few cake designs for our more melancholy shared experiences. This cake, in muted blues and grays, would be the perfect way to say: I know things are bad, but hey, at least we've got cake.

///

Position a rack in the center of the oven and preheat to 200°F.

Clouds

Fill a piping bag fitted with a large round tip with meringue. Line a cookie sheet with parchment paper. Pipe an assortment of clouds onto the parchment paper that range from 2 to 4 inches long. Slide a lollipop stick up through the bottoms of some of the clouds. Return any un-piped meringue to the bowl.

Monogram and Raindrops

STEP 1: Divide the remaining meringue among small bowls. Tint the meringue in each bowl a different pastel rainbow color.

STEP 2: Fit five piping bags with couplers. (Using couplers is optional, but recommended. Swapping one tip quickly between each color will make the job move much faster.) Fill each bag with a different color.

➡

6-inch round cake, finished in pale blue-gray vanilla buttercream

Meringue (page 86)

Pink, blue, yellow, green, and purple gel food coloring

Lollipop sticks

Piping bags

Large round piping tip

Medium round piping tip

Couplers (optional)

Small bowls and spatulas

Parchment paper

Poor penmanship? Type the letter in the font of your choice, make it mega-sized, print it out, and slide it under the parchment paper to use as a template.

UNICORN thought

STEP 3: Place the medium round tip on the bag filled with pale blue meringue. Pipe your desired letter, about 3 inches tall and 2 inches wide. Insert as many lollipop sticks as needed up through the bottom of the letter. Letters like M or N are easier to work with if you use two sticks.

STEP 4: Move to a clear space on the parchment paper. Hold the tip just above the surface of the paper. Apply pressure to the bag. As soon as the meringue makes contact with the paper, pull the tip down and away, releasing pressure as you go. Repeat, making at least a dozen blue raindrops. Repeat the piping process with all of your colors. Rinse and dry the piping tip before moving on to the next bag.

STEP 5: Bake the meringue shapes for 60 to 90 minutes, possibly longer depending on the humidity where you live. Meringues are done when they are firm to the touch and no longer tacky. You should be able to easily lift them from the parchment paper without sticking. Place the cookie sheets on a rack to cool. If it is very humid or raining on the day you make the cookies, turn off the oven when the cookies are done, but leave them in there with the door propped open for another 20 to 30 minutes to continue drying out. There isn't any threat of overbaking meringues at this temperature. When in doubt, leave them in to dry out.

CAKEQUATION

RED VELVET BIRTHDAY CAKE
(page 38)

+

ERMINE BUTTERCREAM
(page 58)

+

PECAN TOFFEE
(page 81)

SHOWERS OF LOVE CAKE

All Together Now

Push the letter into the top of the cake, holding it by the sticks so that you don't crush the cookie. Add clouds around the sides and back of the letter. Finish the sides of the cake with a rainbow of raindrops.

Modern Meringue Cake

Meringue, as a decorating medium, has been totally color pigeonholed. I get it. It's light, fluffy, and ethereal, and naturally lends itself to being used in applications that call for pretty pastel shades. But just because something's always been done a certain way doesn't mean that's the only way it can be done. One of my favorite design methods is to take a technique with a strong tradition of being a certain size, shape, or color, and turn it on its head. Sometimes it works, sometimes it doesn't. Trading in gauzy tones for bold brights updates the floral meringue look in a fun, modern way.

😎 **FAUX FABULOUS:** *Purchase premade meringue cookies in various sizes. Tint the cookies using different shades of food coloring spray.*

//

Position a rack in the center of the oven and preheat to 200°F.

STEP 1: Place about one-third of the meringue in a small bowl and tint it yellow. Place another third in a separate bowl and tint it pink. Tint half of the remaining batter orange and the other half green. Pour the colored meringue mixtures into piping bags fitted with couplers. (Using couplers will enable you to use differently-sized piping tips for one color without having to use a new bag. You could make these cookies without couplers, but it would be much messier and more time-consuming.)

STEP 2: Line a cookie sheet with parchment paper. Place a round cookie cutter or juice glass (or anything round) on the parchment paper and trace it with the pencil. Trace 4 to 6 large and 8 to 10 small rounds. These will be used as guidelines for piping your flowers. Make the rounds as large or as small as you'd like. The flowers I piped were 3 to 4 inches wide for the large ones and 1½ to 2 inches wide for the small ones. Flip the paper over onto the cookie sheet.

STEP 3: Place a large star tip onto the pink meringue's coupler, a small round tip onto the bag of yellow meringue, and a small star tip onto the bag of green meringue. Pipe a ring of nickel-sized dots, following the outline of one of the large rounds. Use an icing spatula to smear the dots toward the center of the round. Pipe another ring of yellow dots so that they overlap the smeared bottom half of the first row. Smear

6-inch round layer cake, finished with yellow buttercream

Meringue (page 86)

Orange, yellow, pink, and bright green gel food coloring

Small icing spatula or popsicle stick

Piping bags

Couplers (optional)

Small and large round piping tips

Small and large star piping tips

Parchment paper

Round cookie cutters or juice glass

Small bowls

Pencil

those dots in toward the center. Finish the flower with a star of green meringue in the center. Repeat this piping and smearing process to fill in the rest of the round outlines, adding as many or as few petals as you'd like. Follow the color patterns pictured or create your own. Pipe single dots and stars with any leftover meringue.

STEP 4: Bake the meringues for 60 to 90 minutes, possibly longer depending on the humidity. Meringues are done when they are firm to the touch and no longer tacky. You should be able to easily lift them from the parchment paper without sticking. Place the cookie sheets on a rack to cool. If it's very humid or raining on the day you make the cookies, turn off the oven when the cookies are done, but leave them in there with the door propped open for another 20 to 30 minutes to continue drying out. There isn't any threat of overbaking meringues at this temperature. When in doubt, leave them in to dry out.

All Together Now

Arrange the meringue flowers to create a whimsical pattern all around the sides of the cake; stand up a few on top. Meringues will begin to soften the longer they sit against the buttercream, so assemble the cake shortly before serving.

When tinting your meringues, be a lazy baker and don't mix the color all the way solid. Leave streaks behind to give the flowers depth and variation.

CAKEQUATION

BANANA CAKE
(page 46)

+

STRAWBERRY-WHITE CHOCOLATE GANACHE INFUSION
(page 64)

+

CANDIED COCONUT CRUNCH
(page 80)

+

YOUR FAVORITE VANILLA BUTTERCREAM
(page 55)

MODERN MERINGUE CAKE

UNICORN thought

Chapter 9

....

CHOCOLATE

MMMM, CHOCOLATE. SOME OF MY VERY FAVORITE decorating techniques appear in this chapter, like the ones for making chocolate flowers. Gorgeous blossoms that also taste divine— what's not to like? Even if you're new to chocolate, give one of these projects a whirl. Start with coating chocolate. Once you're comfortable with that, move on to skills like tempering and chocolate wraps. When you see your first chocolate orchid or pop-art heart fully assembled, and then taste it, you'll be hooked. Chocolate is truly magic. Art for the eyes and the taste buds.

CHOCOLATE CODE OF CONDUCT

Chocolate is a beautiful, delicate, delicious, and wonderful thing. It is also an obstinate goody two-shoes. Chocolate will break your heart if you don't follow its rules. The chocolate rules are not complicated, but deviating from them will turn your silky smooth deliciousness into a chunky, gloppy, streaky mess. Please don't let that stop you from playing with chocolate! I promise you that the small learning curve at the beginning will be only a tiny bump on your road to glossy, crisp, chocolate-decoration goodness.

One of the great benefits of mastering the art of chocolate work (or mastering the art of cutting open a bag of coating chocolate) is that chocolate design elements can be made in advance and stored in an airtight container in a cool, dark place, leaving you plenty of time to primp and chill on the day of your party.

😎 **FAUX FABULOUS:** *Just use coating chocolate and call it a day. No judgments here! Every technique I demonstrate in this chapter works with either. Your chocolate secrets are safe with me.*

CHOCOLATE VS. COATING CHOCOLATE: *What the heck's the difference?*

While many of the same techniques can be used when working with either chocolate or coating chocolate, they're not the same thing. Consider the pros and cons of each before choosing one to use in your next decorating project.

CHOCOLATE (AKA: Couverture)	COATING CHOCOLATE (AKA: Candy Melts or Confectionary Coating)
Made with cocoa butter	Made with vegetable fat
Requires tempering (see opposite page)	Can be used immediately after melting in the microwave in a heatproof bowl on medium-high for 20- to 30-second intervals. Stir the coating chocolate after each round until it's smooth.
Superior flavor (if you're into that sort of thing)	Very sweet, sugary flavor
Needs to be tinted with oil-based food coloring or colored cocoa butters	Comes in a variety of colors. Can also be tinted with oil-based food coloring or candy colors.
Food of the gods	Available at big box stores

TEMPER, TEMPER

I understand that tempering chocolate seems like an intimidating task. I was terrified to do it myself until I gave it a go and realized there's nothing scary going on here at all.

What does "tempering chocolate" mean?

Chemically, chocolate is made up of crystals. The crystals we're concerned with during tempering are the beta crystals. When you start with tempered chocolate, the beta crystals are interlocked and neatly lined up. When you melt the chocolate, those crystals begin to move around and dissipate. Tempering, the process of slowly raising and then lowering the temperature of the chocolate, creates more of those good beta crystals and helps get them back into line. If the chocolate is overheated or cooled too quickly, they don't have the opportunity to properly line back up, and the chocolate will harden without being tempered.

Why do I have to do it?

Chocolate needs to be tempered so that it remains stable at room temperature. Properly tempered chocolate is glossy and snaps with a hard crack when you break it. Untempered chocolate will bloom (develop white streaks), have a dull, matte finish, and bend easily at room temperature. You might think you can cheat the system and just keep your chocolate piece in the fridge, and while that will work for a time, eventually the fridge's humidity will catch up with you and ruin the surface of the chocolate (see "No Water Allowed" on page 184).

Law of Chocolate Physics

★ If you only make as many X as you need (X = petals, dots, hearts, etc.), you will break a number of X as you assemble your design.

★ If you make extra, you won't break any.

★ Always make extra. Unused X can be melted and reused (or eaten).

Do I have to?

I have a secret for you. Well, the first part isn't a secret. Chocolate comes to you already tempered. How awesome is that? The elves at the chocolate companies have to temper the chocolate before pouring it into bars or disks to be shipped, displayed, and sold at room temperature. Here's the secret: You can get away without tempering chocolate if you melt it low enough and slow enough. If you keep your melted chocolate from exceeding 118°F for dark chocolate and 105°F for milk chocolate, you're good to go with no added steps.

If you aren't down for 20 minutes of staring at a bowl of warm chocolate with a digital thermometer to make sure it doesn't fall out of temper (hey, sometimes I am), then the seeding method of tempering is for you. There are a few ways to temper chocolate, but I prefer seeding because it's easy to master and requires no special tools.

Seeding Method for Tempering Chocolate

1. Melt chocolate in a double boiler over medium-high heat. Or, melt chocolate in a heatproof bowl in the microwave on medium for 20 seconds at a time, stirring after each interval. Remove the bowl from the stove or microwave when only a few tiny, rounded pieces of chocolate remain in the melted mixture. Don't let the chocolate exceed 120°F.

2. Stir the chocolate with a rubber spatula, scraping the sides and bottom of the bowl until the remaining chunks have melted. Check the chocolate's temperature with a candy thermometer. If you're at or below the magic numbers—118°F for dark, 105°F for milk or white—then you're good to go.

3. If you're still too warm, add a few pieces of unmelted chocolate to the bowl. Stir again, scraping the sides and bottom of the bowl, until the added pieces have melted. Check the temperature again. Repeat this process as many times as needed to lower the temperature of the chocolate into the ideal range.

4. Repeat the melting and tempering process every time the chocolate hardens or as you need more chocolate.

NO WATER ALLOWED

There is one point that chocolate and coating chocolate agree on: Water is the enemy. Make sure you melt chocolate or coating chocolate in bowls that have been thoroughly dried. Water will cause either to seize into a clumpy, ugly mess. If your chocolate seizes, it can no longer be tempered. However, seized chocolate can still be eaten. Chop up seized chocolate to bake into cookies or use it to make hot chocolate.

No water = no fridge. I know, total bummer! But keeping finished chocolate or coating chocolate pieces in the fridge for an extended period of time will only cause them harm. Refrigerators generate their own level of humidity to help keep fresh foods from drying out. This well-intentioned feature works beautifully for produce, but not so much for chocolate. Eventually, condensation will form on the surface of the chocolate piece, causing it to pit, bloom, and even dissolve if you leave it in there long enough. (Gross!) It's okay to sneak pieces into the fridge or freezer for a few seconds at a time to speed up the hardening process, but tempered chocolate doesn't need it. Allowing it to set up at room temperature ensures a clean product every time.

UNICORN thought

Save chocolate chips for baking cookies. The chocolate I use when decorating is called couverture. It has a higher percentage of cocoa butter than chips or baking chocolate. Couverture comes in bar, disk, or chunk form. To make sure you're purchasing couverture, a good rule of thumb is to look for chocolate that lists the cocoa percentage on the package.

OOOOH, SHINY

Something that chocolate and I have in common is a preference for shiny things. When making chocolate decorations, applying melted chocolate to a shiny surface (like acetate or foil) before leaving it to dry will encourage the chocolate to harden with a shiny finish. Acetate is a kind of thin, flexible plastic that you can purchase at cake decorating stores or online. Using something with a porous or matte finish, like parchment paper, will cause the chocolate to dull a little. It's not the biggest deal unless your friends and children are accomplished pastry chefs, but in that case, why aren't *they* making the cake?!? The only time acetate is truly the preferred tool is when making large pieces that will have to be moved (acetate is much sturdier) or when making decorations that require shaping after the chocolate is spread (foil and acetate can both do the job).

Keeping Melts Melty

An annoyance of working with coating chocolate is keeping it melted and fluid as you're working with it. Its quick-set qualities are great for whipping up decorations in a pinch, but can be frustrating when working with multiple colors. Here are a few tips for keeping things melty.

» Instead of taking trips back and forth to the microwave when working with multiple colors of coating chocolate, pour the coating chocolate chips into paper cups. Nestle the cups together inside a slow cooker set on low heat. Stir the chips every so often until completely melted.

» Keep piping bags full of coating chocolate smooth and fluid by storing them on a heating pad set to high while you work. Protect the pad with a paper towel and top with foil to hold in the warmth. Use the same heating pad to soothe your aching back after a day of caking.

8-inch round layer cake, finished in smooth, pale pink buttercream

Additional 2 cups pink buttercream, in a piping bag fitted with a large star tip

3 cups yellow coating chocolate or chopped tinted white chocolate

1 cup each pink and purple coating chocolate or chopped tinted white chocolate

Small star cookie cutters

Small round cookie cutters

Small icing spatula or popsicle stick

Spoon

Small frying pan

Toothpick or skewer

Parchment paper

Piping bag

Assorted complementary sprinkles (gold stars, metallic sprinkles, pink and yellow pearls, etc.)

Find tips for working with chocolate and coating chocolate on page 182.

Lucky Star Cake

Who says planets and stars and celestial bodies can't exist in pastel, cotton-candy shades? Not this unicorn! If you're a stickler for accuracy, by all means choose colors that better reflect reality. But if you (or someone you love) happen to adore rainbow colors, glitter, and star gazing, then these colors are for you.

Earn bonus points by making extra shooting stars and planets. Use them to garnish cake slices along with a smattering of celestial-themed sprinkles. Too hot to bake? Just make some planets and stars and use them to top intergalactic ice cream sundaes.

😎 **FAUX FABULOUS:** *Swap in star-shaped candies and gumballs for stars and planets. Pop a gumball into a ring-shaped gummy candy for a Saturn stand-in.*

//

Shooting Stars

STEP 1: Melt the yellow coating chocolate. Dip the end of a small icing spatula (or popsicle stick) into the melted chocolate. Smear the chocolate in an arcing motion onto a piece of parchment paper. Lift the icing spatula up and away from the paper toward the end of the arc to create the jagged edge of your shooting star's tail. Go over the arc a few times to create a wider tail. Repeat as many times as you'd like, creating arcs in various widths and lengths. The ones on this cake are 1 to 2 inches long. Set the tails aside to dry while you make the stars and planets.

STEP 2: Pour a few spoonfuls of melted yellow chocolate onto a separate piece of parchment paper. Hold the paper by the edges and wiggle it a little to help the candy flatten and spread. Pop the puddle of coating chocolate into the fridge for 5 to 10 minutes, or until it has hardened.

STEP 3: Warm a small, empty pan over low heat. Hold the cutting edge of one of the small star cookie cutters against the surface of the warm pan for just a few seconds. Use the heated edge to cut shapes from the hardened coating chocolate. (Warming the cutter first allows it to easily cut through the solid candy.) Repeat with the other star

★ No tiny round cookie cutters? No problem. Use the tops and bottoms of round piping tips.

★ Turn your galaxy into a unicorn (or kitty, dinosaur, puppy, etc.) galaxy by creating a few molded mini chocolate shapes using the technique in step 4 of the Unicorn Carousel Cake (page 189). Add the shapes to your mix of chocolate pieces, sprinkles, and candy.

UNICORN thought

PULL HERE!

cutters, rewarming as necessary. Wipe the cutters between cutting and rewarming to prevent any stray chocolate bits from burning. Set some stars aside to use without tails.

STEP 4: Attach stars to their tails by dabbing a drop of melted chocolate onto the back of a star before placing it on the pointed end of a tail. Allow the finished shooting stars to set up completely before placing them on the cake.

Planets

STEP 1: In separate bowls, melt the pink and purple coating chocolate. Repeat the same pouring and cutting process as in previous steps 2 and 3, but with the small round cutters. Make some solid-colored rounds and some marbled rounds. Create the marbled rounds by pouring spoonfuls of two different shades of melted chocolate next to each other. Swirl the colors together using a toothpick or skewer.

STEP 2: Fill a piping bag with melted purple chocolate. Snip the tip off the bag. Pipe rings onto some of the planets. Allow the rings to set up completely before placing them on the cake, about 5 minutes.

All Together Now

Pipe S-shaped swirls of buttercream around the top and bottom edges of the cake. Top the swirls with shooting stars, planets, and a dusting of assorted sugar pearls and metallic sprinkles.

CAKEQUATION

STRAWBERRY CAKE
(page 46)

➕

WHITE CHOCOLATE-COATED SUGAR COOKIE CLUSTERS
(page 88)

➕

LEMON CURD
(page 65)

➕

LEMON BUTTERCREAM
(page 61)

LUCKY STAR CAKE

Unicorn Carousel Cake

My sister started referring to me as a unicorn when she worked for me at my wedding cake shop. It started as a joke when an overly affectionate customer came in gushing about me and the cakes. Sarcasm is our love language, so with an eye roll and smirk, she instantly christened me "the unicorn." The joke snowballed and I decided to embrace my new identity—flowing mane, sparkly horn, and all. A unicorn bust now hangs over my daughter's crib. It's never too early to learn about your heritage.

If unicorns aren't your thing, this is still a festive and fun cake decorated as a classic carousel in either pastels or primary colors. Create the traditional horses to encircle the cake, or go wild and add jungle animals.

😎 **FAUX FABULOUS:** *Skip the fancy chocolate work and replace the molded chocolate figures with frosted animal crackers.*

//

STEP 1: Press 10 of the swirled candy sticks evenly around the sides of the cake. It's okay (and encouraged) if the some of the sticks overlap the ganache drips.

STEP 2: Melt the pink coating chocolate. Dip a Sixlet into the melted chocolate and set it on top of one of the candy sticks. Repeat with the rest of the sticks.

STEP 3: Press the remaining candy stick into the center of the top of the cake. Dip the pink gumball in the pink chocolate and place it on top of the stick. You may have to hold it there for a minute to keep the gumball steady.

STEP 4: Place both unicorn cookie cutters on a parchment-lined cookie sheet. Pour a spoonful of melted pink chocolate into each cutter. Gently tap the cookie sheet against your work surface a few times to help the chocolate smooth, spread out, and fill in the small spaces. Pop the cookie sheet into the fridge for just a minute or two. Remove the sheet and carefully release the chocolate figures from the

→

6-inch round layer cake, finished with sprinkle-speckled buttercream (see page 104) and a pink ganache drip (see page 103)

1 cup each pink, yellow, blue, green, and purple coating chocolate or tinted white chocolate

11 yellow and blue swirled hard candy sticks

Large pink gumball

10 pink Sixlets or candy pearls

Unicorn cookie cutter (3 inches)

Unicorn cookie cutter (2 inches)

Parchment paper

cutters. If you lose a leg, tail, or horn in the process, don't panic! Dip the broken edge in melted chocolate and reattach it to the unicorn. Use the tip of your finger to smooth over any chocolate that pops up over the seam. Set the pink unicorns aside and repeat the process using the small unicorn cutter with the yellow, blue, green, and purple coating chocolates. Make two of each color so that you have 10 small unicorns total.

All Together Now

Flip over the large unicorn and spread a small amount of melted chocolate vertically down the center of its body. Pick up the unicorn and press it against the candy stick topper. Hold it steady for a minute until it's solidly attached. Use the same technique to attach the smaller unicorns to the candy sticks at varying heights around the sides of the cake.

CAKEQUATION

FUNFETTI BIRTHDAY CAKE
(page 34)

+

STRAWBERRY BUTTERCREAM
(page 61)

+

LEMON MERINGUE
(page 86)

UNICORN CAROUSEL CAKE

6-inch round layer cake, finished in smooth yellow buttercream

Additional 1 cup yellow buttercream

2 cups white coating chocolate or white chocolate, chopped

2 cups each black and red coating chocolate or chopped tinted white chocolate

Heart cookie cutter (3 inches wide)

Heart cookie cutter (1½ inches wide)

Piping bags or paper cones

Small icing spatula

Parchment paper or acetate

Black permanent marker

Ruler or straightedge

Find tips for working with chocolate and coating chocolate on page 182.

Pop-Art Heart Cake

Part of the fun of working with chocolate is learning to think about designs in reverse and in layers. This modern pop-art design showcases the technique of layering piped chocolate pieces in an updated, whimsical way. It's also a great cake to make for someone who's totally over pastels and piped flowers.

Keep this cake in mind if you've got a little superhero in your house. Change up the design and create word bubbles to say things like *WOW!*, *BAM!*, or a happy birthday message. It's a simple, chic alternative to printed images and plastic figurines, and way more economical than an over-the-top sculpted cake.

😎 **FAUX FABULOUS:** *Save your precious digits the aches and pains and use mini chocolate chips instead of piping dozens of dots.*

Hearts

STEP 1: With the marker, trace the outline of the 3-inch-wide heart cookie cutter three times on a piece of parchment paper. Space the hearts 4 to 5 inches apart to give yourself room to work. On a separate piece of parchment paper, trace the outline of the 1½-inch-wide heart six times, spacing those hearts out as well. Flip over the parchment paper so that the chocolate doesn't come into contact with the marker.

STEP 2: Melt the black coating chocolate. Fill a piping bag or cone with the melted chocolate. Snip the tip off the bag and use it to fill in one of the large and two of the small heart outlines. Repeat with the red coating chocolate, filling in one of the large and one of the small heart outlines. Set the filled hearts aside to harden.

While the black chocolate is still soft, move to a new piece of parchment paper and pipe approximately 60 to 70 tiny dots, about the size of a pea. Set aside to harden.

STEP 3: In a small heatproof bowl, melt together 1 cup of the white coating chocolate with two disks of the black coating chocolate. Stir the melted chocolate until it's solid gray in color. Pour the melted

chocolate into a piping bag. Snip the tip off the bag and use it to fill in one of the small heart outlines. Set aside to harden, about 5 minutes.

STEP 4: Melt the remaining 1 cup white coating chocolate. Fill a piping bag with the melted chocolate. Snip the tip off the bag and use it to pipe arcing teardrop shapes in the last large and two small heart outlines. Pipe the teardrop opposite to the side you'd like the final drop to appear. For example, I piped my drops on the right side of my heart outlines so that the glint of light would appear on the left side of my finished hearts. Keep what remains in the piping bag nearby to help with assembly.

STEP 5: Assemble the large heart first. Use a small icing spatula to help lift the large black chocolate heart off the parchment paper and then flip it upside-down. Next, do the same with the large red heart. Adhere the red heart to the black heart using a few dabs of melted chocolate (it doesn't matter which color because you won't see it). Offset the red heart so that the rounded side of the heart, where you'll be placing the white teardrop, allows a little more black to peek through. Last, carefully flip over the large teardrop. Adhere the drop to the red heart using a dab of melted white chocolate. Repeat the same assembly process to complete the gray heart and smaller red heart. Allow the hearts to harden completely before placing them on the cake.

STEP 6: Arrange the piped dots, flat-side out, on the sides of the cake in a Swiss dot pattern: Start the first row by placing a dot on the buttercream just above the bottom of the cake. Place the next dot below the top edge of the cake, directly above the first dot. Add a third dot between the first two dots. Place another dot between the top and middle dots. Add the last dot between the bottom and middle dots. Use a ruler or straight-edge if you need a guide, but I always prefer to eyeball my Swiss dot patterns. No cake is ever exactly the same height

UNICORN thought

Too much caffeine this morning? Warm the tip of a small knife with a blow-dryer. Use the warm knife to clean up any wobbly edges.

all the way around. I've always believed it's better for a cake to look right to the eye than to be exactly symmetrical.

Place a second row of dots in the exact same pattern, approximately 2 inches away from the first row. Imagine that the top two dots in the first row and the top two dots in the second row form a square, and place a dot directly in the middle of that square. Move down the line, adding dots in the center of each square. Repeat this pattern around the entire cake.

All Together Now

Attach the hardened hearts (sounds so sad for such a cheery cake!) by using a small icing spatula to smear dabs of buttercream onto the back of each piece. Press the chocolate pieces onto the side of the cake with firm, steady pressure. Make sure the back of each piece comes into contact with as much buttercream as possible. This is especially important to help keep the large heart in place. Chill the entire cake in the fridge for 20 minutes, or until the buttercream has firmed up and the chocolate pieces are set in place.

CAKEQUATION

CHERRY CAKE
(page 46)

+

MINI CHOCOLATE CHIPS

+

CHOCOLATE BIRTHDAY CAKE
(page 37)

+

RASPBERRY JAM
(page 68)

+

YOUR FAVORITE VANILLA BUTTERCREAM
(page 55)

POP-ART HEART CAKE

Lux Layers Cake

This is one of those cake designs where the sum is truly greater than its parts. Sanding sugar, sprinkles, nonpareils, and coating chocolate are all common ingredients, but combine them in a thoughtful and innovative way, and you have a shimmering, couture masterpiece. The only premium ingredient here is your time.

I stuck with a clean black and white palette, but this design can be reimagined in endless ways, like the cake on the title page. Go bold with brights, or soft and ethereal with pastels. It's an ideal cake for a birthday party, baby shower, or bridal shower—easy and inexpensive, yet sparkly and impressive.

STEP 1: Place a piece of parchment paper over the flower template and trace the flower with a black marker, or draw a flower freehand. Flip the paper over so that the candy doesn't come into contact with the marker lines. Open the clear sanding sugar and keep it nearby.

STEP 2: Melt the white coating chocolate and pour it into a piping bag. Snip the tip off the bag and fill in the entire flower outline. Quickly, while it's still wet, dust the entire surface of the flower with clear sanding sugar. Set the flower aside to harden, about 10 minutes.

STEP 3: Draw three 3-inch-long leaves and at least two dozen 1-inch-long leaves on a piece of parchment paper. No need to get overly precise with this—just eyeball the sizes, making three leaves larger than the rest. Flip the paper over. Open the black nonpareils and black sparkling sugar and keep them nearby.

STEP 4: Melt the black coating chocolate and pour it into a piping bag. Snip the tip off the bag and fill in one of the large leaf shapes. Dust the entire surface of the leaf with black sparkling sugar. Repeat this

→

6-inch round layer cake, finished in white buttercream encrusted with clear sanding sugar (see page 104)

Small amount additional buttercream, for attaching flowers and leaves

4 cups each black and white coating chocolate or white and dark chocolate

1 cup clear sanding sugar

2 cups black nonpareils

2 cups black sparkling sugar

1 cup gold sprinkles

Parchment paper

Piping bags or paper cones

Black permanent marker

Flower template (page 226), optional

Find tips for working with chocolate and coating chocolate on page 182.

If at any point your chocolate hardens before you add the sprinkle party, don't freak out. Just pipe over the area and work a little faster this time. Chop, chop.

UNICORN thought

process with the rest of the large and small leaves. Do the larger leaves one at a time, but the smaller leaves can be done a few at a time. Set all the leaves aside to harden, about 10 minutes.

STEP 5: Use the piping bag filled with the black coating chocolate to outline the petals of the flower and add detail lines to the centers of the petals. While the candy is still wet, dust the black lines with black nonpareils. Don't worry about getting nonpareils on other parts of the flower, as they'll only stick to the melted chocolate. Set the flower aside to harden, about 10 minutes.

STEP 6: Finish the leaves by piping an outline around the edges, plus a center line and smaller detail lines on the larger leaves. While they're still wet, dust the lines with black nonpareils. Set the finished leaves aside to harden while you finish the flower, about 10 minutes.

STEP 7: Working on a cookie sheet, carefully turn over the flower to shake off any stray nonpareils. Return leftover nonpareils to their container. Remove any stubborn nonpareils with the tip of a knife or skewer.

STEP 8: Pipe stamens onto the center of the flower with the black coating chocolate. While they're still wet, dust the stamens with gold sprinkles. Set the flower aside to harden, 5 to 10 minutes.

All Together Now

Attach the large flower to the cake by smearing a few dabs of buttercream onto the back of it. Press the flower against the side of the cake with firm but gentle pressure. Tuck the larger leaves in behind the flower, using buttercream to help them stick to the back of the flower and to the cake. Add the tiny leaves along the bottom edge.

CAKEQUATION

BLACK VELVET BIRTHDAY CAKE
(page 38)

+

HAZELNUT MERINGUE
(page 86)

+

BLACKBERRY CABERNET BUTTERCREAM
(page 61)

LUX LAYERS CAKE

Fa La La Cake

I would put a Christmas tree in every room if it wouldn't drive my husband crazy and if my kids didn't dismantle things 10 seconds after they're assembled. I can never decide on a single design direction during the holiday season. Modern, traditional, pastels, retro—I love them all! Since I'm not quite ready to become the Christmas-trees-up-year-round lady, and because I end up hunting under beds and in toy bins for most of my decorations thanks to little hands, I just cram all my holiday design goals onto cakes.

This design can be tweaked in a number of ways to match your holiday aesthetic. I went with plastic-y brights to satisfy my modern holiday cravings. Choose deeper colors for a more traditional look, or simply use the chocolate pieces with the shiny side down. Make leaves and letters in shades of blue with silver accents for a non-holiday wintery feel.

Leaves

STEP 1: Draw two horizontal lines 3 inches apart on a piece of acetate with the marker (or on parchment paper with a pencil). Flip the paper over to avoid having any of the melted chocolate come into contact with the markings.

STEP 2: Melt the light green coating chocolate in a small heatproof bowl and pour it into a piping bag or cone. Snip the tip off the bag and use it to pipe freehand squiggly-edged leaves, using the space between the lines as your guide for length. Make at least 24 leaves. Set the leaves aside to harden while you work on the rest of the components. Reserve what's left in the piping bag to use for the letters.

STEP 3: Repeat the process in step 1, except space the lines 1½ inches apart. Repeat the process in step 2, but this time use the darker green coating chocolate to pipe simple holly leaves. (Pull up a picture of holly online to use as a guide if needed.) Make at least 16 holly leaves. Set them aside to harden while you work on the rest of the components.

8-inch round layer cake, finished with white buttercream (see page 99)

2 cups each pink and light green coating chocolate

1 cup each dark green, blue, purple, yellow, orange, and red coating chocolate

Black permanent marker (or pencil if using parchment)

Acetate or parchment paper

Ruler

Heavy-duty aluminum foil

Small bowls

Small icing spatula

Thin knife with at least a 3-inch-long blade

Piping bags or paper cones

Find tips for working with chocolate and coating chocolate on page 182.

Fa La La La La La La La La

STEP 1: In a small heatproof bowl, melt the blue coating chocolate and pour it into a piping bag. Snip the tip and use it to pipe a FA and a LA. Repeat this same (tedious but necessary) process to create LAs in purple, yellow, pink, and orange. Allow all of the letters to harden completely before using them on the cake. The letters are thin and delicate, so pipe more than you'll need to account for breakage.

STEP 2: Fill a piping bag with melted red chocolate and pipe 18 large pea-sized mounds. Allow the mounds to harden completely before using them on the cake.

Poinsettia

STEP 1: Tear off a 2- to 3-inch-wide piece of foil. Using the same bag of melted yellow coating chocolate from step 1 above, pipe 10 pea-sized dots onto the aluminum foil. Set the dots aside to harden or pop them in the fridge to speed up the process, just a minute or two.

STEP 2: Tear off five 2-inch-wide strips of aluminum foil. Cut the strips into pieces approximately 3 inches long. Fold the pieces in half lengthwise and open them back up.

STEP 3: Dip the flat side of a small knife into the melted pink chocolate so that about 2 inches of the knife is coated. Lay the coated side of the knife onto one of the pieces of foil (open-side up) so that the tip of the knife lines up with the crease in the foil. Pull the knife away, smearing the chocolate onto the foil in a petal shape. Rock the knife back and forth until your desired petal shape is achieved. Repeat this process 11 times so that you have at least 12 large bracts total. As always, it's a good idea to make more than needed to account for breakage.

STEP 4: Repeat step 3 to make the smaller, inner bracts, but this time, dip the knife so that only about 1 inch is coated with chocolate. Make at least five small bracts.

Have a little fun with your partygoers and slip a LOL or Say Whaaat? in with your Fa La La's and see if anyone notices. You just might start a new tradition.

UNICORN thought

→

STEP 5: Tear off a 6-inch-wide piece of foil. Push the piece of foil into a small bowl to create a little cup. Spoon a small quarter-sized puddle of melted pink chocolate into the center of the cup. Place the flat end of a large bract into the puddle of chocolate. Repeat with five more bracts, overlapping the edges as you go.

STEP 6: Spoon another smaller puddle of melted chocolate into the center of the first layer of bracts. Arrange the smaller bracts the same way you laid out the larger bracts in step 5.

Add more bracts between the two layers to fill in any gaps. Break bracts as needed to fill in smaller spaces. Dip the flat end of a bract into the melted chocolate. Slide it into place, making sure the melted chocolate makes contact with the rest of the flower, "gluing" it into place.

UNICORN thought

Add another dimension to this cake design by getting fancy with frosting. Decorate the sides of the cake with vertical stripes that match the shades of the Fa La Las.

STEP 7: Spoon a dime-sized puddle of melted pink chocolate into the center of the small bracts. Drop the tiny yellow flower centers into place, arranging them in a circular cluster. Set the finished flower aside or pop it in the fridge until hardened, about 10 minutes.

All Together Now

Place the poinsettia on top of the cake toward the edge. Use a small icing spatula to help lift all of your piped components off the acetate or parchment paper and flip them over. Arrange both kinds of leaves (shiny, flat-sides up) around the outer edge of the top of the cake, like a wreath. Add the holly berries and letters to finish the design.

CAKEQUATION

**CHOCOLATE
STOCK CAKE**
(page 48)

+

**BAILEYS
BUTTERCREAM**
(page 61)

+

**CANDY-COATED
PRETZEL
CLUSTERS**
(page 89)

FA LA LA CAKE

Spring in Bloom Cake

Spring flowers are my favorite of the whole year. Late winter and early spring can be especially gray here in New Hampshire. The time between the last snow and when the first buds show their faces can seem like a slushy, muddy eternity. When the first blooms open, I do a little happy dance and hide my snow boots, looking forward to the brighter, warmer days ahead.

This cake is a chocolate lover's dream, perfect for any springtime celebration! Change the design to suit any season by swapping the flowers and colors to match what's in bloom around you.

😎 **FAUX FABULOUS:** *Short on time but want a cake with a similar look? Make these store-bought swaps:*

» *Green licorice twists for the stems*

» *Black licorice drops for the daisy centers*

» *Almond slices for the daisy petals*

Find more inspiration from the Sweet Bouquet Cake (page 114).

///

STEP 1: Cut the bendy ends off your straws if they have them. Cut the straws in half lengthwise, creating two long, curved open pieces. Set the cut straws on a cookie sheet, curved-side up.

In a small heatproof bowl, melt the light green coating chocolate and pour it into a piping bag. Snip the tip and use it to fill the straw halves with chocolate. Allow the stems to harden completely before using them on the cake, about 10 minutes.

STEP 2: Melt the yellow coating chocolate. Dip the flat side of the small knife's blade into the melted chocolate, coating about 2 inches of the blade. Hold the knife above a piece of parchment paper and line up the spot where the chocolate stops with the edge of the paper. Press the knife against the paper, and then pull it down and away. Repeat many times, making four to six petals for every daisy. Set the petals aside to harden completely before using, about 5 minutes.

For the leaves, repeat the same process using the larger knife and the green coating chocolate. Make at least 16 leaves.

6-inch round layer cake, finished in chocolate buttercream (page 60) or ganache (page 62)

Additional 1 cup ganache

2 cups each yellow, purple, and white coating chocolate

2 cups light green coating chocolate

1 cup black nonpareils

1 dozen plastic straws

Small icing spatula

Small knife

Medium-sized knife, or steak knife

Heavy-duty aluminum foil

Plastic spoons

Parchment paper

Scissors

Tiny scooper or melon baller

Find tips for working with chocolate and coating chocolate on page 182.

STEP 3: Melt the purple coating chocolate. Dip your squeaky-clean thumb into the chocolate and use it to spread chocolate inside the well of a spoon. Repeat as many times as needed to solidly coat the inside of the spoon. Repeat, making at least three petals for every tulip. Set the spoons aside and allow the chocolate to harden completely before using, about 10 minutes.

STEP 4: Melt the white coating chocolate. Re-melt the yellow and purple chocolates if they've begun to harden. Dip the tip of your finger into one of the colored chocolates and press it against a piece of parchment paper. Quickly pull it down and away, smearing the chocolate into a tiny petal shape. Dip the tip of your thumb into the same color and create another petal the same way, only larger this time since you're using a bigger finger. Make three small petals and two large petals for every pansy. To make petals with variegated colors, allow the first layer to harden before pressing a second color onto the petal. Allow the top edge of the first color to peek through. Set the petals aside to harden, about 5 minutes.

STEP 5: Spoon a pea-sized dot of melted chocolate the same color as your petals into the well of a foil-lined plastic spoon. Place a large pansy petal onto the spoon so that the tip of the petal rests in the chocolate. Place another large petal next to the first, overlapping the edges. Lay a small petal on top of the first large petal, then another small petal on top of the second large petal. Add a final small petal

opposite the first two, creating a small triangle. Set the assembled flower aside to harden, about 5 minutes. Repeat the process with the rest of the pansy petals.

All Together Now

Carefully slide the green chocolate stems out of the straws. Place the chocolate stems around the sides of the cake at varying heights.

Use a small scoop or melon baller to make a tiny ball of ganache. Roll the ball of ganache in black nonpareils, and then cut it in half. Place the cut side of one of the balls against the cake at the top of a chocolate stem. Use a small icing spatula to help lift the yellow daisy petals off the parchment paper. Insert petals into the ganache center all the way around, four to six petals per center. Repeat to make as many daisies as you'd like.

Scoop another tiny ball of ganache. Press the entire ball against the cake at the top of a chocolate stem. Arrange two tulip petals over the ball of ganache, overlapping the edges. Add the petals with the pointier ends facing up.

Press leaves into the sides of the cake alongside the chocolate stems. Arrange pansies around the bottom edge of the cake.

CAKEQUATION

ALMOND BUTTER CAKE
(page 40)

➕

LEMON SHERRY BUTTERCREAM
(page 61)

➕

CANDIED ALMOND CRUNCH
(page 80)

- - - - - - - - - - - - - - - -

SPRING IN BLOOM CAKE

6-inch round layer cake and 8-inch round layer cake, stacked and finished with a pink and white watercolor buttercream finish (see page 103)

8 cups chopped white chocolate or coating chocolate

Pink and green colored cocoa butter (or oil-based food coloring or colored coating chocolates)

Heavy-duty aluminum foil

Apple shipping crates or small bowls

Plastic spoons

Skewer

Fine-tipped paintbrush

Small offset spatula (optional)

Find tips for working with chocolate and coating chocolate on page 182.

Wedding Bells Cake

Don't worry, you don't have to wait until your wedding day to make this cake! I call it the Wedding Bells Cake because of the peony. When I owned my cake shop, peonies were my thing. Not chocolate ones (at the time), but delicate gum paste ones. I handcrafted them, petal by painstaking petal, and they became my calling card. One summer a few years ago, I looked up and realized I couldn't remember a cake in recent history that didn't have one. We looked back through the orders and, sure enough, I was on cake number 40-something containing at least one sugar peony. It was that summer that I thought to myself, "Self! Boy, I sure wish people could actually eat these little beauties. Especially with all of the time and hard work that goes into making them . . . " That's when the lightbulb went off. The wires in my brain crossed, and my fine pastry background intersected with my high-end cake shop experience. The answer was chocolate. Isn't it always?

When making flowers from gum paste, you roll the sugar dough first and then use tools to create impressions in the dough that mimic real flower petals. When working with chocolate, the process is reversed. You must make the form and apply the chocolate to it, working from the outside-in. Heavy-duty aluminum foil quickly became my best friend. It's inexpensive, malleable, and leaves chocolate with a beautiful shine. Trust me, spring for the good stuff. Regular aluminum foil is too flimsy and weak for the job. Apple shipping crates may also seem like an oddly specific supply, but they're actually quite useful—and typically free. Stalk the produce guy at your local supermarket and ask if you can take the apple crates once they're done emptying the boxes. It's trash to them, so they usually happily hand them over. The wells in the crates are the perfect size for molding large, cupped petals.

See the pretty peony on a single tier, page x.

Peony

STEP 1: Tear off a 5-inch-wide sheet of aluminum foil. Press the foil into one of the apple crate's wells (or into a small bowl). Repeat until all of the wells are lined, or until you have at least a dozen crinkled foil cups. Don't worry about keeping the foil smooth—it's the wrinkles that we're after! They give the chocolate petals their ruffled, realistic look.

Tear off a 3-inch-wide sheet of aluminum foil. Rip that sheet into three equal pieces. Use one of the pieces to line the well of a plastic spoon, wrapping the excess foil around the edges of the spoon. Repeat until you have six lined spoons total.

STEP 2: Melt and temper (see page 183) a little more than half of the white chocolate. Dip your immaculately clean thumb (or the tip of a small offset spatula) into the melted chocolate and use it to spread a thin layer inside one of the foil cups. Keep the coverage spotty and sparing. This layer is just to add a little depth of color to the outside of the petals. Repeat with the rest of the foil cups and spoons.

STEP 3: Melt the pink cocoa butter and add it to the melted white chocolate a few drops at a time, until you achieve your desired shade of pink. Re-warm and re-temper as needed. Use that same spotless thumb to spread a thicker layer of pink chocolate into the foil cups and spoons. Swipe your thumb up and around the sides of the cups to create each petal's shape. Fill the lined spoons and cups so that no foil shows through. Set all the petals aside until the chocolate has hardened, about 10 minutes.

STEP 4: You are going to make a mess. Please, don't worry about it; it's part of the fun. Also, don't wear your actual wedding dress while making chocolate flowers. An apron is safer.

Carefully remove the chocolate petals from their foil backings. Use some of the foil to re-line one of the apple crate cups (or a small bowl). Pour a quarter-sized puddle of white or pink chocolate into the bottom of the cup. Place a large petal into the cup so that one end of the petal sits in the melted chocolate. Add more petals, filling the perimeter of the bowl and overlapping the edges as you go. Continue to add more petals to the interior of the flower. As the flower fills in, it will be tougher to get petals to reach down to that bottom puddle of chocolate. Fill in any gaps by dipping the edges of a petal in chocolate before sliding it into place. The melted chocolate will help the petal adhere to the petals around it. Use the smaller petals created on spoons for the center of the flower. Break petals as needed to fit them into place. Set your finished flower aside to harden completely before using, about 10 minutes.

→

Make extra petals well in advance to use as cake slice garnishes. Store them in airtight containers in a cool, dark place.

UNICORN thought

Leaves

STEP 1: Tear off a 5-inch-wide piece of foil. Tear the sheet into four smaller pieces. Stack the pieces and cut them into the shape of a leaf. Peel the stack apart. Place one of the foil leaves in the palm of your hand. Use a skewer to score a center line detail. Flip the leaf over so that the indent you created is facing up. Repeat with the other leaves.

STEP 2: Melt and temper the remaining white chocolate. Melt the green cocoa butter and stir in a few drops at a time until your desired shade of green is achieved. Spread the green chocolate over the leaf forms. Drape the coated leaves over the edges of the apple crate to dry. Shape them to resemble the way real leaves hang. Set aside to harden, about 10 minutes.

STEP 3: Peel the leaves away from their foil backings. Use the paintbrush to lightly coat the surface of each leaf with melted green cocoa butter to give it a more realistic appearance. Set the leaves aside to allow the cocoa butter to dry, 5 to 10 minutes.

All Together Now

Use the edges of the foil to lift the peony out of the apple crate. Place the cup in the palm of your hand and carefully peel away the foil. Gently press the peony into place so that it sits on the top edge of the bottom tier, facing out. Tuck in the leaves so that they stick out above and below the peony.

CAKEQUATION

ORANGE CLOVE BIRTHDAY CAKE
(page 34)

+

HONEYCOMB CANDY
(page 84)

+

YOUR FAVORITE VANILLA BUTTERCREAM
(page 55)

WEDDING BELLS CAKE

Potted Orchid Cake

You don't need me to tell you that this potted chocolate orchid cake is a stunner. Make one and you're sure to knock everyone's socks off. Put the cake on the table, drop the mic, and strut out of the room. You'll be the stuff of legends.

The orchid is also the namesake of my former wedding cake shop, Wild Orchid Baking Co.—the wild vanilla orchid, to be specific. It's the source of—you guessed it!—the vanilla bean. After discovering its intoxicating properties, the Totonacs of Mexico created an intense, romantic, and teensy bit morbid tale of star-crossed lovers to explain the vanilla orchid's origin. The old *deity-falls-for-a-silly-human* story. I'll save you the gore and cut to the good part: It ends with the vanilla orchid being their gift of love to the world. What could be better than naming my shop after one of my most often-used ingredients, which also comes with such an incredible story? The name helped to set the tone for what people came to expect from my cakes: clean, modern designs with a touch of romance and whimsy.

 FAUX FABULOUS: *Skip the fancy wiring and fill the top of your chocolate pot with a simpler flower, like the pansies on page 204 or the peony on page 209.*

Chocolate Wrap

STEP 1: In order to wrap your cake in chocolate, you'll need a piece of acetate that's as wide as your cake is tall and a few inches longer than the cake's circumference. The circumference of a 6-inch round cake is a little less than 19 inches, so you'll need to tape two sheets together. Measure your sheet by wrapping it around the cake to double-check the size.

➡️

6-inch round layer cake, crumb-coated

6 cups chopped white chocolate or coating chocolate

2 cups chopped dark chocolate

Black, gold, green, and yellow cocoa butter (or oil-based food coloring or colored coating chocolates)

1 cup chocolate cookie crumbs

3 cloth-covered 16-gauge floral wires

Green floral tape

Heavy-duty aluminum foil

Piping bag

Parchment paper

Acetate

Offset icing spatula

Small knife

Apple shipping crates or small bowls

Skewer

Fine-tipped paintbrush

Scissors

Tape

Needle-nose pliers

1 smoothie straw

Find tips for working with chocolate and coating chocolate on page 182.

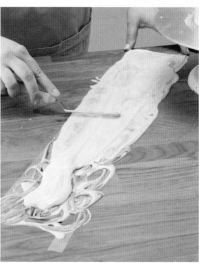

STEP 2: Melt 3 cups of white chocolate. No need to temper for this technique; the chocolate will remain fluid longer if it is untempered, and it will also be much easier to cut the finished cake. Melt the black cocoa butter and keep it nearby. Pour the melted white chocolate onto the acetate sheet and, using an offset spatula, spread it out to the edges. Splatter a few drops of the black cocoa butter onto the white chocolate and swirl the colors together.

STEP 3: Use the pieces of tape to help lift up the sheet and wrap it around the chilled, crumb-coated cake. Start at one end, pulling the sheet around the cake as you go. Run your hand over the sheet to make sure all of it comes into contact with the buttercream. The end of the sheet should overlap the beginning of the sheet by a few inches. Don't press the overlap onto the start of the sheet. Make sure the chocolate is touching and let any excess just hang off the side of the cake. You'll trim it away once the wrap has set up. Pop the cake in the fridge until the chocolate has hardened, about 15 minutes. Be patient! Removing the wrap too soon will damage your chocolate finish.

Use a blow dryer to gently soften chocolate wraps that harden too quickly.

UNICORN thought

STEP 4: Remove the cake from the fridge and peel off the acetate sheet. Use a knife to score a line where the ends of the wrap overlap. Gently apply pressure, running the tip of the knife up and down that line until it cuts through. Remove the extra chocolate. If you accidentally cause any breakage, just reattach the broken piece of chocolate using a little white chocolate to secure it in place. Disguise any cracks or patches in step 5.

STEP 5: Using a fine-tipped paintbrush and melted gold cocoa butter, add metallic details to the finished marble wrap.

Wire Form

STEP 1: Gather three pieces of wire. Keep one piece whole and cut the other two in half.

STEP 2: Use needle-nose pliers to bend the end of one of the shorter wire pieces into a nickel-sized circle. Twist the bent end of the wire together with the long part of the wire to secure the loop. Repeat with two more of the short wire pieces.

STEP 3: Using floral tape, attach all of the shorter wire pieces to the long wire. Each short piece will need to be taped on individually. Start with the short, straight piece and tape it to the long wire so that the ends of wire are staggered an inch or two apart. The distances don't need to be exact; the wires are meant to mimic real orchid stems and vines.

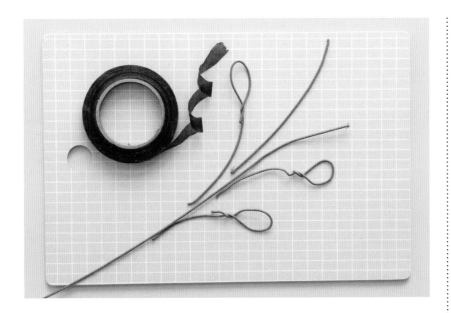

Tear off a piece of floral tape that's about 6 inches long. Pull each end of the tape at the same time to stretch it and activate the stickiness. Tightly wrap the tape around the wires, spinning the wires between your fingertips and pulling the tape taught against the wires. Repeat the same process to attach the looped wires to the long center wire. Space them a few inches apart as you move down the wire. Set the whole wired contraption aside while you work on the flowers.

Phalaenopsis

Buds

STEP 1: Lay the wired stem on a piece of parchment paper. Melt and temper 2 cups of white chocolate. Melt the green cocoa butter and pour a few drops into the tempered white chocolate. Stir to combine, adding more until your desired shade is achieved. You'll be painting green cocoa butter directly onto the buds and leaves at the end, so the green chocolate base color doesn't have to be very dark. Aim for a light green shade.

STEP 2: Pour about ½ cup of the green chocolate into a piping bag. Pipe a 1-inch-long almond shape onto the ends of both un-looped wires. Mound up the chocolate a bit in the center of the almond. Allow the chocolate to harden before continuing, about 10 minutes.

STEP 3: Flip over the wires and pipe chocolate onto the back of each almond shape, mounding chocolate up toward the center. Set the wires aside and allow the chocolate to harden completely before using, about 10 minutes.

Leaves

STEP 1: Tear off three 3-inch-wide pieces of aluminum foil. Push one of the foil strips into the well of an apple crate. Remove the foil from the well and flip it over, cup-side down. Repeat with the other foil pieces.

STEP 2: If it has hardened, re-melt and temper the green chocolate. Pour some of the melted chocolate into a piping bag. Pipe a long, teardrop-shaped leaf onto the foil form. Pipe it so that the fat end of the teardrop sits over the cupped part of the foil. Repeat, making two more leaves (three total). Allow the leaves to harden completely before coloring, about 10 minutes.

STEP 3: If it has hardened, re-melt the green cocoa butter. Paint the melted cocoa butter onto the leaves and buds to deepen the color and add dimension. The cocoa butter will set up very quickly, in less than a minute or two.

Large Rounded Petals

STEP 1: Tear off a 3-inch-wide sheet of foil. Cut the sheet into three equal pieces. Cut one of the pieces into three long rectangles and set aside. Push each of the two larger pieces into the well of an apple crate. Repeat this process two more times, for a total of six large cupped pieces and nine small rectangular pieces of foil.

STEP 2: Melt and temper 2 cups of white chocolate. Dip your clean thumb into the chocolate and smear it onto one of the cupped pieces of foil. If you don't want to use your hands, use a paintbrush instead. Swipe your thumb back and forth, like a windshield wiper, creating a rounded triangular shape. Repeat the same process on the remaining cupped pieces of foil (six total).

Long Pointed Petals (Sepals)

Fold the rectangular pieces of foil from step 1 of the rounded petals in half lengthwise and open them back up. Dip the flat side of a small knife into the melted white chocolate to coat about 2 inches of the blade. Lay the coated side of the knife onto one of the pieces of foil (open-side up) so that the tip of the knife lines up with the crease in the foil. Pull the knife away, smearing the chocolate onto the foil in a petal shape. Repeat this process eight more times so that you have nine petals total.

Tiny Inner Petals (Throat)

Dip the tip of your pointer finger (or a popsicle stick) into the white chocolate. Press your coated finger against a piece of parchment paper. Then, quickly pull it down and away, smearing the chocolate in a tiny petal shape. Repeat eight more times so that you have nine tiny petals total.

→

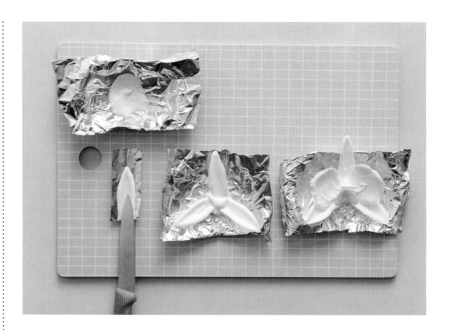

Assemble the Flowers

STEP 1: Tear off a 4-inch-wide piece of foil. Tear the sheet into three equal pieces. Use each piece to line a well of the apple crate. Pour a nickel-sized puddle of white chocolate into one of the lined wells. Carefully peel away the foil from three of the pointed inner petals. Place the flat end of each petal into the chocolate puddle in a triangle shape. Arrange the petals so that the bottom two are just shy of being horizontal and the middle one sticks straight up. Repeat the process with the rest of the pointed petals, making two more orchid bases.

STEP 2: Carefully peel the foil off two larger rounded petals. Add a pea-sized puddle of white chocolate to the center of the pointed petal triangle. Place the tip of each petal into the chocolate puddle. Arrange the petals so that the rounded edges sit between two pointed petals on either side. Use the tip of a knife or small icing spatula to lift three tiny petals off the parchment paper. Place the three tiny petals into the puddle, almost sticking straight up and facing each other in an upside-down U-shape. Repeat the entire process to assemble the other two orchids. Set all the flowers aside to harden completely, about 15 minutes.

STEP 3: Melt the yellow cocoa butter. Using a fine-tipped paintbrush, add details to the center of each flower. The cocoa butter will set up very quickly, in about a minute or two.

STEP 4: Pick up one of the orchids by the foil. Place it in the palm of one hand. Gently peel off the foil and lift the flower away from it. Set it aside. Repeat with the other flowers. If any of the petals break during the unfolding process, dip the broken edge of the petal into melted white chocolate and reattach it to the flower. Smooth over the seam with the tip of your finger.

STEP 5: Push the looped parts of the wired stem flat against a piece of parchment paper. Pour white chocolate into one of the wire circles, allowing some of the chocolate to run outside the lines. Place one of the orchids onto the puddle of chocolate. Repeat this process with the other circles and orchids. Allow the flowers to harden completely on the wires before moving the finished stem, at least 10 minutes.

All Together Now

Insert a smoothie straw into the center of the top of the cake. Trim the top of the straw to be level with the top of the cake. Carefully pick up the chocolate orchid stem and insert the wire into the smoothie straw. The straw will protect the cake from coming into contact with the wire. Delicately bend the wire so that the stem arches over the side the cake, falling like a real orchid. Fill the top of the cake with the chocolate cookie crumbs. Arrange the leaves around the base of the stem. Secure them in place with a dab of chocolate on the backs of the leaves.

CAKEQUATION

NUTELLA CAKE
(page 40)

+

CANDIED HAZELNUT CRUNCH
(page 80)

+

MILK CHOCOLATE GANACHE
(page 62)

+

YOUR FAVORITE VANILLA BUTTERCREAM
(page 55)

POTTED ORCHID CAKE

Oooh, Charts

HOW MANY SERVINGS? -

The serving recommendations in this chart for the round and square pans are based on tall cakes that consist of 4 layers of cake and 3 layers of filling, cut into slices that are approximately 5 inches tall by 1 inch wide by 2 inches deep. Shorter cakes of the same size and shape will serve less. Serving totals for a loaf pan, classic bundt cake, and sheet cake have been included for your convenience.

	6-INCH	8-INCH	9-INCH	10-INCH	12-INCH
Round	12 servings	24 servings	28 servings	38 servings	56 servings
Square	32 servings	50 servings	n/a	50 servings	72 servings
9-inch loaf			9 servings		
Bundt			12 to 16 servings		
Sheet, single layer	9 × 14: 24 servings	11 × 15: 36 servings	12 × 18: 54 servings		

HOW MUCH BATTER? -

Yields for the cake recipes in this book are provided in cups. This chart explains how many cups of batter you'll need to fill round and square pans to bake tall layer cakes. The measurements are based on filling 3-inch-tall pans a little more than halfway full. Batter amounts for a classic bundt cake, sheet cake, and cupcakes have been included for your convenience.

	6-INCH	8-INCH	9-INCH	10-INCH	12-INCH
Round	4 cups	5 cups	7 cups	12 cups	18 cups
Square	6 cups	9 cups	n/a	18 cups	28 cups
9-inch loaf			5 cups		
Bundt	10 cups				
Sheet, single layer	9 × 14: 18 cups	11 × 15: 26 cups	12 × 18: 32 cups		
Cupcakes	¼ cup per liner				

HOW MUCH FILLING? —

This chart explains how many cups of filling you'll need to fill different size cakes. Keep in mind that softer fillings (jam, ganache, pastry cream) will require extra buttercream to pipe a dam around the filling (see page 96). The measurements are based on filling cakes that consist of 4 layers of cake and 3 layers of filling. When I fill a cake, I aim for 1-inch-high cake layers and ½-inch-high filling layers.

CAKE SIZE	FILLING AMOUNT
6-inch round	2 cups
8-inch round	4½ cups
10-inch round	7½ cups
12-inch round	10 cups
6-inch square	3 cups
8-inch square	6 cups
10-inch square	9 cups
12-inch square	12 cups

HOW MUCH FROSTING? —

This chart explains how much frosting (buttercream, ganache, cream cheese, etc.) you'll need to crumb coat and finish different size cakes. Make more if you plan on adding frosting design elements (piping, ruffles, etc.).

CAKE SIZE	FROSTING AMOUNT
6-inch round	4½ cups
8-inch round	5½ cups
10-inch round	7 cups
12-inch round	9 cups
6-inch square	6 cups
8-inch square	8 cups
10-inch square	10 cups
12-inch square	12 cups

Conversion Charts

PAN SIZES

US	METRIC
6 in.	15 cm.
8 in.	20 cm.
10 in.	25 cm.
12 in.	30 cm.

TEMPERATURE

FAHRENHEIT	CELSIUS	GAS MARK
200°	93°	¼
250°	120°	½
300°	150°	2
325°	165°	3
350°	175°	4
400°	205°	6

VOLUME

US	METRIC
1 tsp.	5 ml
1 Tbsp.	15 ml
1 oz.	30 ml
¼ cup	60 ml
⅓ cup	80 ml
½ cup	120 ml
⅔ cup	160 ml
¾ cup	180 ml
1 cup	240 ml

WEIGHT

US	METRIC
¼ oz.	7g
½ oz.	14g
1 oz.	29g
1½ oz.	43g
2 oz.	57g
4 oz.	113g
8 oz.	227g
1 lb.	454g
2 lb.	904g
4 lb.	1.8kg

COMMON INGREDIENT WEIGHTS - - - - - - - - - - - - - - - - - -

INGREDIENT	US	METRIC
1 cup all-purpose flour	5 oz.	145g
1 cup cake flour	4.5 oz.	130g
1 large egg (no shell)	1.75 oz.	50g
1 large egg white	1.05 oz.	30g
1 large egg yolk	0.65 oz.	18.6g
1 cup butter	8 oz.	227g
1 cup vegetable shortening	6.75 oz.	191g
1 cup vegetable oil	7.7 oz.	218g
1 cup heavy cream	8.2 oz.	232g
1 cup sour cream	8.5 oz.	242g
1 cup buttermilk	8.5 oz.	242g
1 cup whole milk	8.5 oz.	242g
1 cup water	8.3 oz.	236g
1 cup granulated sugar	7 oz.	200g
1 cup packed dark brown sugar	8.4 oz.	239g
1 cup packed light brown sugar	7.7 oz.	217g
1 cup confectioners' sugar	4 oz.	115g
1 cup honey	11.75 oz.	336g
1 cup molasses	11.25 oz.	322g
1 cup corn syrup	11.5 oz.	328g
1 teaspoon baking powder		4.9g
1 teaspoon baking soda		5g
1 teaspoon kosher salt		6.7g
1 teaspoon powdered gelatin		3.1g
1 teaspoon vanilla extract		4g
1 cup cocoa powder	3.33 oz.	95g
1 cup peanut butter	8.8 oz.	250g
1 cup almond paste	10 oz.	284g
1 cup almonds	2.6 oz.	75g
1 cup pecans	4 oz.	114g
1 cup walnuts	4 oz.	114g
1 cup hazelnuts	5 oz.	142g
1 cup chocolate chips	6 oz.	175g

Templates

FLORAL CROWN CAKE
(page 149)

 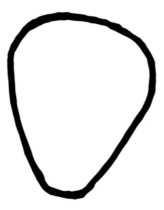

CAN YOU DIG IT? CAKE
(page 154)

LUX LAYERS CAKE
(page 197)

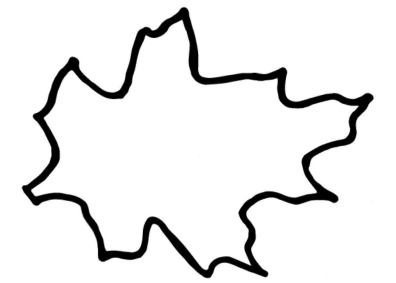

AUTUMN CRISPS CAKE
(page 146)

CAN YOU DIG IT? CAKE
(page 154)

AUTUMN CRISPS CAKE
(page 146)

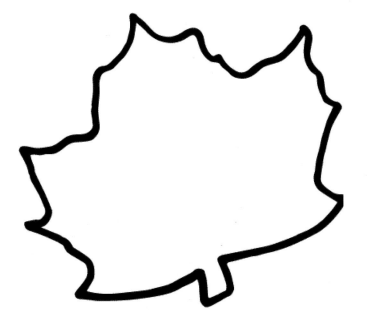

Resources

GLOBALSUGARART.COM

» One-stop resource for cake and cookie decorating supplies: cutters, food coloring, ingredients, piping tips, pans, etc.

JBPRINCE.COM

» Popular chef's resource. Great place to find interesting molds, serving pieces, and cutting-edge equipment.

KINGARTHURFLOUR.COM

» Wonderful resource for ingredients and baking information.

AMAZON.COM

» Gotta love Prime, right? Find just about anything baking- and pastry-related when you need it by 3 p.m. tomorrow.

ETSY.COM

» Lots of small shops offering unique and custom cutters and molds.

WILLIAMS-SONOMA.COM

» Reliable measuring cups, spoons, and other baking tools.

CANDYWAREHOUSE.COM

» Great for bulk candy purchases and tracking down hard-to-find candies.

CHEFRUBBER.COM

» A pastry chef's resource. Chocolate tools, molds, cocoa butters, acetate, flavorings, food coloring, and more.

BAKEDECO.COM

» Large selection of baking supplies (pans, cake boards, cupcake liners, etc.) and higher-end pastry tools (chocolate work, molds, etc.).

HEDLEY & BENNET

» Makers of the adorable pink apron I'm wearing throughout this book.

FLOUR CONFECTIONS

» A great source for unique items, specialty tools, and dragees in fun shapes.

WILTON

» Find piping tips, bags, cookie cutters, candy melts, and more on Wilton.com or in the baking aisles of craft stores.

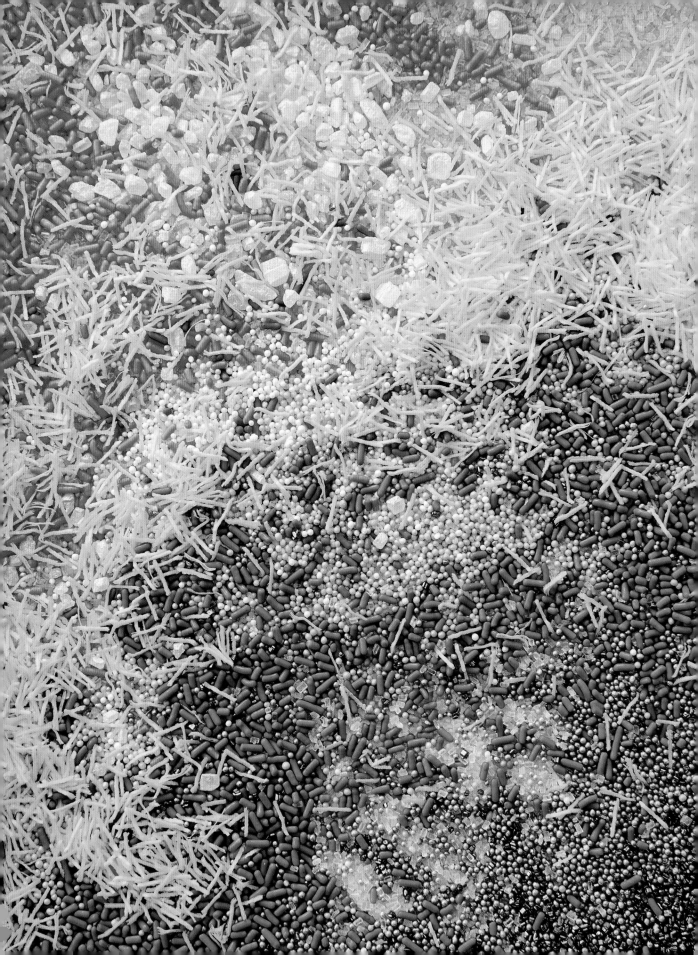

Acknowledgments

TO MIKE, THANK YOU FOR YOUR UNCONDITIONAL LOVE AND SUPPORT.
For putting up with buttercream everywhere and too many cake stands. For being the best father, partner, and friend I could ever ask for. Hearts.

To Maxwell and Violet, my little muffins: Max, thank you for always being curious about what Mommy is making and telling me it's beautiful every time, no matter what. Your curiosity and hunger for knowledge inspire me every day. Violet, my wild child, thank you for being my little snuggle bear throughout this entire process. And thank you for not breaking too many things while Mommy was working.

To Dervla Kelly, my editor, thank you for thinking I knew what I was doing. ;) I sincerely appreciate your excitement and encouragement throughout this process. Thank you for your confidence in me and in this book.

To Alison Fargis, my agent, thank you for your dedication in bringing this book to life, as well as your generous advice, encouragement, and honesty. I can't thank you enough.

To Rae Ann Spitzenberger, thank you for humoring my strange requests and last-minute additions. Most of all, thank you for bringing my thoughts and recipes to life in such a beautiful way. You totally nailed it.

Thank you to Mitch Mandel, Troy Schnyder, Naomi Storey, and the Rodale Test Kitchen crew for your invaluable help in bringing so much joy and color to the pages of this book. Stephanie Hanes, thank you for reading my mind and making choices that perfectly illustrate my style.

To Heath Robbins, Paul Rutherford, Verne Cordova, Sharon Lupo, Katherine Hennessy, Katrin Schippering, and Monica Mariano: Thank you for your hard work in creating many of the gorgeous images in this book.

To everyone at Rodale who has worked to make this book a success: Anna Cooperberg, Andrea Modica, Alisa Garrison, Deri Reed, Angie Giammarino, and Susan Turner—thank you!

To Carrie Sellman at *The Cake Blog*, and Karen Kelty, Kristen Doherty, and the entire team at *Craftsy*, thank you for giving me a platform to share what I love do. Your feedback and support make me a better communicator. Thanks for understanding all the missed deadlines and late posts (who, me?!).

To my students and readers, thank you for your tremendous support, trust, and encouragement over the years, and for keeping me on my toes, asking great questions, and making me a better writer and instructor.

Index

Flowers: Floral Crown Cake (page 149)
Leaves: Can You Dig It? Cake (page 154)